Vegetable Gardening

By the Editors of Sunset Books
and Sunset Magazine

Lane Publishing Co., Menlo Park, California

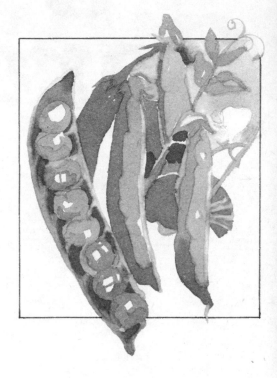

Acknowledgments

For their helpful advice and assistance, we wish
to extend special thanks to: Gerald F. Burke,
Donald Bruce Johnstone, Klaus Neubner, Elmer
G. Twedt, and Charles B. Wilson.

Supervising Editor: Patricia Hart Clifford
Research and Text: James W. Wilson

Special Consultant: Joseph F. Williamson
                    Garden Editor, Sunset Magazine

Design and Illustrations: Dick Cole

Cover: Photograph by John Flack

Executive Editor, Sunset Books: David E. Clark

First Printing, February 1975

Contents

Special Features

Which Vegetables are for You?

Vegetables are as individual as the people who grow them. Radishes are for people in a hurry; endive is for salad lovers; pumpkins are for people with big backyards; carrots are for nibblers. Before you decide which vegetables to grow, ask yourself a few questions to find those most compatible with you.

Most importantly, which vegetables do you like to eat? These, along with the favorites of the people your garden will feed, will be at the top of your list. Then ask yourself if you have the time to prepare these vegetables for canning or freezing or if you just want to grow enough to eat freshly picked. This will determine not only the varieties you choose but also whether you will plant all at once for a big harvest or plant every few weeks.

(Continued on page 6)

Giant pumpkins *like this 'Big Max' variety demand lots of room.*

Closely-spaced lettuce *thrives in mounded beds, benefits from organic soil preparation methods (see page 35).*

Yardlong beans *offer delicious change of pace, take a small amount of attention (see page 60).*

Ruffly rhubarb *goes as well in the flower garden as it does in a rhubarb pie (see page 90).*

Container crops *on sunny deck include cucumbers (upper left), tomatoes, carrots, and radishes (see page 7).*

(Continued from page 4)

Consider, too, your space and time. If your space is very limited, you might just try a tomato plant in a pot and a tub of salad greens. Unless you have a large space, avoid relatively cheap staples or space-consuming crops, such as potatoes, melons, and rhubarb. The size of your garden depends also on how much time you have for such chores as watering and weeding. Initially, you'll put in more time preparing the soil and planting, but once this is done, plan to spend about 15 to 30 minutes a day taking care of a 10 by 10-foot garden. Remember that some crops demand more attention than others. If your time is limited, avoid those that require tying up or frequent feeding.

And finally, consider the climate of your area. Some vegetables are frost tender; some are hardy. Some like it cool, and some like it hot. Check the Gardener's Guide, pages 56-95, to find out when to work a particular vegetable into your planting schedule.

PLAN AHEAD

The arrival of seed catalogs by mail and the appearance of seed racks in stores signal the time to start planning your garden. Both the catalogs and the seed displays appear in time for early spring sowing of slow-starting seeds indoors.

What's your climate like?

When you select the vegetables you will grow, consider two climate factors. The first is frost tenderness. The length of the growing season for frost-tender vegetables is determined by two dates, the last spring frost and the first fall frost. Plan to grow frost-tender vegetables only in the period between the two average dates for your area. (See page 33 for average frost dates.)

The second important climate consideration is the temperature preferred by the vegetable—warm or cool. Even when the danger of frost is past, warm-season vegetables need adequate heat to germinate the seed, set fruit, and ripen their crops. Cool-season vegetables will usually recover from a moderately heavy frost and can be grown throughout the winter in mild climates. These grow poorly when it's hot.

With most warm-season vegetables, the fruit is what you harvest (tomatoes, squash, melons, peppers, eggplant); with most cool-season crops you harvest the leaves, roots, or stems (lettuce, spinach, carrots, broccoli). Seeds of warm-season crops will not sprout and plants will not grow if the weather is not warm enough for them; cool-season crops will bolt in warm weather, producing premature flowers and seeds instead of the leaves, roots, stems, or immature flowers that you want to harvest.

If you think your climate is too cool for the crops you want to grow, try early varieties—they require less heat to mature than late varieties. Some warm-season vegetables, however, require so many warm days and nights that they rarely succeed in northern states.

Carefully consider your climate and the beginning of the frost-free period before deciding *when* to plant. Don't assume that because seeds or plants of a particular vegetable are on display it's the best time for setting them in your garden. Dealers sometimes offer frost-tender plants too early for safe planting. Check the Gardener's Guide (pages 56-95) to find out if a plant is tender or hardy and whether it grows better in cool or warm weather. This will tell you when to plant that vegetable.

Once you know the climate requirements and length of the growing season of a particular plant, you might find that spring may not be the best time to plant some vegetables. In warm regions, for example, autumn is the best season for planting cool-season vegetables. And to avoid harvesting an overabundance of vegetables over a short period of time, plan for successive small plantings of many crops. Good timing is one of the key secrets to successful vegetable gardening.

Include some perennials

Only a few vegetables will come back reliably for several seasons, sending up new growth from heavy, frost-hardy roots: asparagus, horseradish, Jerusalem artichoke, multiplying onion, and rhubarb. (Jerusalem artichoke, a native American relative of the sunflower, is grown for its starchy tubers. The true artichoke is a perennial only where winters are mild.)

Don't confuse these true perennials with annual plants that give you volunteer seedlings each spring from seeds dropped the previous year. Tomatoes, for example, are prolific reseeders. Volunteer plants can be grown to harvest, but they may not look or perform like their parents.

Climbers save space

Plant-for-plant, pole (climbing or runner) types often yield twice as much as bush varieties. Some people claim that pole varieties have more flavor than bush kinds.

Plan on training the vines up supports such as stakes, tepees, or frames. You'll need 8-foot-long, 2 by 2-inch stakes for individual plants. For several plants, use 8-foot long 4 by 4-inch stakes as posts, running wire and heavy string between them. Tepees can be made of lightweight stakes or bamboo poles (see page 8).

In very hot climates, don't use metal frames, chicken wire, or galvanized clothesline wire for stringers. Plant leaves and tendrils can burn from touching the hot metal.

Only pole beans and tall peas actually cling. Beans cling strongly with spiraling, twining vine tips; peas

(Continued on page 9)

Container crops

If you are short on tillable ground, you might try growing vegetables in containers. Large wooden boxes, barrels cut in half, pressed pulp tubs, and large clay pots all make practical containers deep enough for all but the very largest vegetables. If a container doesn't have drainage holes, drill them into the bottom and cover them with pieces of clay pot or rock so the soil doesn't run out with the water. Besides not allowing enough root room, containers that are too small dry out too fast and are easily tipped over.

Fill the containers with a porous, fast-draining soil mix. A heavy soil does not absorb water readily enough or drain fast enough to promote good root formation. A heavy soil mass will also tend to shrink away from the sides of the containers so that water will pour down the sides of the dry root ball rather than penetrating it. Use a commercial mix or make your own with one part garden loam, one part river sand, and one part leaf mold or peat moss.

If you use an artificial soil, such as U.C. mix, add lime and superphosphate to correct acidity and guarantee that sufficient phosphorus will be immediately available to the roots. (Add 5 to 8 pounds dolomitic limestone and 2 to 3 pounds superphosphate per cubic yard of soil.) Incorporating up to one-quarter soil into the mix will supply micronutrients not contained in the other ingredients and will add beneficial soil organisms.

To maintain steady growth, feed vegetables weekly with a fertilizer such as fish emulsion, diluted as directed on the label, or use a controlled-release fertilizer that provides the nutrients for the entire growing season from a single application. Check the soil for moisture daily—containers will probably need watering at least that often in hot weather.

Check the Gardener's Guide, pp. 56-95, to find if a vegetable you want to grow would be successful in containers. Consider, too, the following points when deciding which crops to grow: 1. If the containers will be on display, the plants should be attractive, even during harvest. Fruiting plants, such as tomatoes, peppers, and eggplant, fall into this category, as well as such plants as Swiss chard that continue to grow even though outer leaves are harvested. 2. Select crops, such as radishes, lettuce, and chives, that grow quickly so you can harvest them and replant another crop in the same container. 3. Choose vegetables that yield a satisfying harvest from one or two plants. It would be impractical to use a number of containers for just one meal.

Compact 'Patio' *variety tomato plant suits containers perfectly, shows off tasty tomatoes.*

Dill, basil, *and a couple of 'Blue Lake' pole bean plants decorate the patio and supply the kitchen.*

Give your climbers a lift

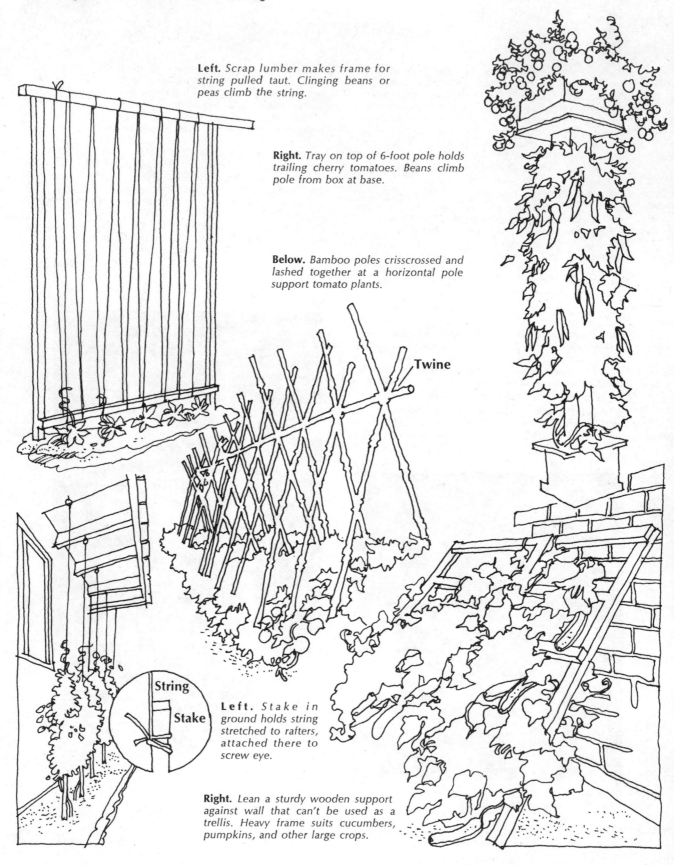

Left. *Scrap lumber makes frame for string pulled taut. Clinging beans or peas climb the string.*

Right. *Tray on top of 6-foot pole holds trailing cherry tomatoes. Beans climb pole from box at base.*

Below. *Bamboo poles crisscrossed and lashed together at a horizontal pole support tomato plants.*

Twine

String

Stake

Left. *Stake in ground holds string stretched to rafters, attached there to screw eye.*

Right. *Lean a sturdy wooden support against wall that can't be used as a trellis. Heavy frame suits cucumbers, pumpkins, and other large crops.*

Ladder *keeps pumpkin vine off the moist ground, saves space.*

Recycled Christmas tree *transformed into a bean pole provides inspiration to use what you have on hand to support climbers.*

(Continued from page 6)
cling weakly with special tendrils. Neither plant is entirely self-training and will need occasional tying and tucking in.

A good plan is to run rows of trellised vegetables east and west on the north side of the garden so they don't shade the shorter crops growing near them.

Herbs take little space

If you'd like to try herb gardening, plant a few clumps of herbs to separate long rows of vegetables into short segments. At first, stick to the easily grown flavoring herbs: marjoram, sage, basil, dill, thyme, oregano, and chives. Add different kinds as you learn to appreciate the many subtle improvements that fresh herbs can bring, not only to vegetables but also to many other foods.

LOOK AROUND BEFORE YOU DIG

Vegetables are particular about soil, sun, and water. They grow rapidly during the season that suits their nature and don't like to be starved or stunted by lack of water, nutrients, or sun. Whether you are planting a window box with lettuce or a large garden, consider the basic needs of all vegetables:

• Choose a spot in the sun. A successful garden must have at least six hours of sun a day (preferably full sun). Most vegetables prefer sun all day. The south and west sides of your yard normally get the most light and heat. In hot desert areas, the plot should have afternoon shade. Winter gardens in mild climate areas should have full sun all day.

• Find a sheltered location. In windy climates side-yard gardens particularly can be exposed to blasts of wind so strong that growth is retarded or staked plants are knocked over. This is especially true in urban areas where buildings are closely spaced. However, if this is the only spot for your garden, a windbreak made of clear fiberglass will reduce wind without cutting off sunlight.

• Look for a plot where air can circulate well. Plant diseases thrive in stagnant air. If a cramped space is all that is available, tall, sturdy stakes can carry climbing vines up into the sun and breeze (see page 8).

• Avoid areas under or just beyond overhanging tree branches. Invading tree roots reach out even beyond the foliage canopy to compete for nutrients and water.

• Start your garden about two feet from house walls. Unless you can excavate and replace the soil, you'll find that the ground immediately next to most homes (especially new ones) may contain harmful lime that has seeped down from concrete, stucco, or plaster walls, and concrete foundations.

• Choose an area handy to the water faucet to avoid dragging around long lengths of hose.

• Avoid low areas that flood during heavy rains. Deep, rock-filled sumps bored into the soil can sometimes solve the problem of water standing in low spots.

• Don't rule out areas with sloping ground, such as banks and hillsides. By taking precautions against erosion and sliding of soil, you can produce as many delicious vegetables there as you would on level ground (see page 13). Soil on a hill, however, is more likely to be shallow or more rocky than flatland soil.

• There's no reason to limit your garden to one plot. Small, narrow areas along sunny fences or walls make good locations for climbing or vining vegetables. You also may be able to add small salad crops here and there in beds of flowering plants. Small islands of grass that are bothersome to maintain can become excellent sites for vegetable beds. Drive short pegs or posts in the corners of these plots to keep hoses from knocking down the plants.

If you have scouted your property and can't find a good site for a vegetable garden, don't be discouraged. Look around your immediate neighborhood for idle land on which to plant a garden, such as easements under power transmission lines. (Check to see if you need a permit.) Small businesses sometimes have back lots that are eyesores but can be gardened in return for cleaning them up. And some forward-looking cities rent small vegetable plots for modest fees. Don't depend on

the inherent honesty of people to protect an off-premises garden, though. Passers-by may succumb to the temptation to take vegetables unless you can fence the area and lock the gate.

DRAWING UP A GARDEN PLAN

After you have chosen and measured your garden area, spread out a large sheet of paper—shelf paper will do. Use a simple scale, such as one inch for one foot. Draw lines every 3 inches across the paper to represent walkways 3 feet apart in the plot. Picture the space between

Early spring. *Give plants that have a long growing season an early start by planting as soon after your last frost as the ground can be worked. Asparagus will be in the longest (up to 20 years) so plant it in the back of the garden out of the way. Rhubarb, another perennial, could take the place of artichokes in cold-winter climates. All these crops like it cool.*

Midspring to early summer. *Plant when the soil has warmed up. If they're planted too early, they'll just sit and wait for warm weather. Swiss chard is one of the few leaf crops that will take some heat. If you have a fence at the back of your plot, use it for tying the tomato vines. A support will allow you to space the vines more closely. None of the other vegetables need staking.*

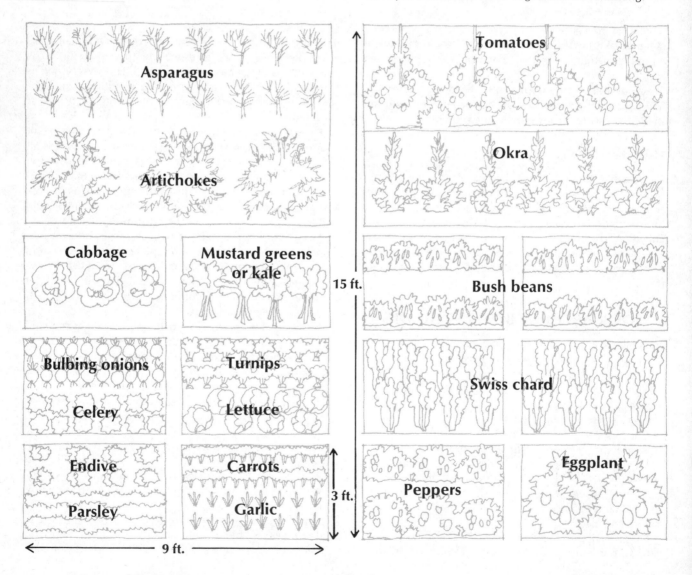

the walkways as slightly raised beds. Down each of these beds you can run two rows of small-to-medium sized vegetables or one row of larger types. Extra-large spreading vegetables, such as melons and squash, must be given two or three full beds to sprawl across. Seed packets give you some clues by listing heights and recommended spacing between plants, but also consider the points that follow.

Visualize mature height and spread

Such perennials as rhubarb and asparagus grow very tall and can be harvested for only a relatively short time.

Late spring to midsummer. *Plant these if you have lots of space. You'll need room for at least three rows of corn to insure adequate pollination. Melons, pumpkins, cucumbers, and squash are all notorious for their space-eating, sprawling vines. Supports for these plants (see page 8) will make best use of space and keep fruit off the damp ground. All these crops need heat.*

They should be placed in the back of your garden so that they're out of the way after harvest. Plant tall vegetables on the north side of the garden and shorter ones on the south side. Sweet corn, pole varieties of beans and peas, and tomatoes are all tall-growing vegetables.

Bush squash and eggplant can reach two and a half feet in height. Place them in the middle of the garden. Most other vegetables—bush beans, beets, carrots, and turnips, for example—grow no more than 14 to 18 inches high and equally wide.

Don't be misled by the descriptive term "bush" when it's applied to summer squash, eggplant, and okra. Bush

Late summer or early spring. *If frost comes late to your area, plant these cool-season crops for a winter harvest. If your winters remain mild, you can make succession plantings until the weather warms up the following spring. Most of these crops will withstand light frosts. In cold-winter areas, plant these crops as soon as the ground can be worked in the spring.*

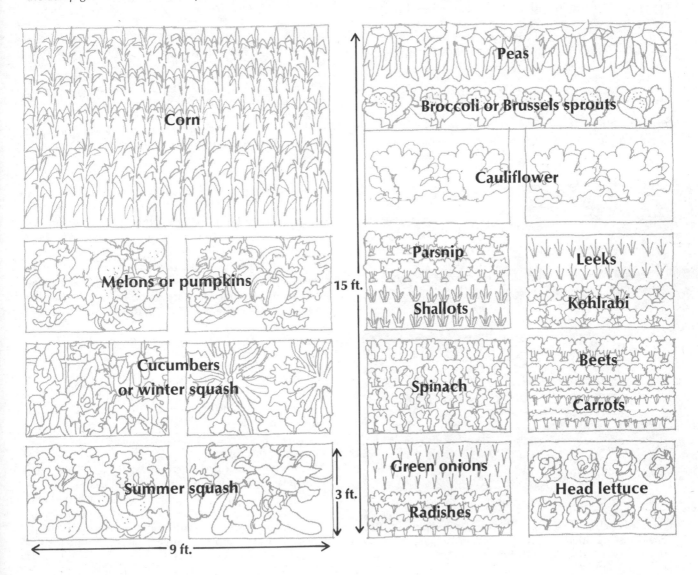

varieties are more compact than the runner types, but even they can grow 30 inches high and 4 feet wide. Another misnomer is "dwarf" okra; in rich soil this plant can grow nearly 6 feet tall by the end of summer. Double-check the mature size of dwarf and miniature vegetables in the seed catalog or on the packet before you buy.

The size of some mature plants, such as Brussels sprouts, cauliflower, and cabbage, is not the same as the size of the heads at produce counters. Outer leaves on late-maturing cabbage, for example, can cover a 24 to 30-inch span. Cauliflower, Brussels sprouts, and broccoli can grow to 24 inches high and equally as wide. Kale and collards don't form heads like cabbage; instead, they develop tall, upright plants.

Think short rows

Divide each row into short segments, about 4 feet in length. This will keep you from planting too much of any one vegetable at a time. Plant long rows of vegetables only if you intend to can or freeze them or if they are a type you can leave on the plants for a while after they mature. Vegetables that can be stored on plants include winter squash, potatoes, turnips, rutabagas, onions, and beans grown for dry seeds.

Interplant to save space

Interplanting lets you harvest more vegetables from a small garden. Instead of planting individual rows of

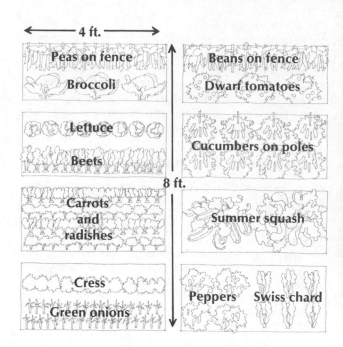

Space-saver garden. *This four by eight-foot garden fits a raised bed, plot in the lawn, or side yard. The plot on the left contains cool-season crops; plant these in succession until the weather warms up and again in the fall if your winters are mild. Onions from sets give you a faster harvest than those grown from seed. As the weather warms, replace the cool crops with transplants of crops on the right, either started indoors from seed or purchased at the nursery. Replant cool crops in fall.*

quick-maturing vegetables (leaf lettuce, radish, curly cress, onion sets, spinach, turnips, and mustard greens), scatter a few of these seeds among young plants of larger or slower-maturing vegetables, such as sweet corn, peppers, tomatoes, and eggplant. Some gardeners never plant separate rows of radishes; they just plant radish seeds among the slow sprouters, such as parsley and carrots. The radishes are eaten before the parsley and carrots are more than an inch or so high.

Plan for successive crops

You can use the same space to grow two or three crops in succession in a single season. Combined with interplanting, succession cropping can help you harvest more from a given area. When you take out an early crop, plant another one as soon as you can work amendments into the soil.

Here's a typical sequence of succession planting: plant peas or spinach in very early spring. As soon as these crops are out of the ground, rework the bed and plant warmth-loving vegetables, such as beans. In mild-winter climates you can pull up the beans and plant carrots, radishes, turnips, lettuce, or cole crops for fall and winter harvests.

Space-saving idea. *Crowd a second sowing of fast-growing vegetables next to mature plants.*

If your land isn't level

If you have a scarcity of level land for growing vegetables, don't despair. It takes a bit more work to prevent soil erosion and keep the water from running downhill, but you can grow vegetables on a slope.

Run the rows on the contour lines of the hill—rows running up and down the hill are difficult to irrigate. If your area receives a great deal of rainfall, pile a stack of compost at the low end of the rows to absorb fast-flowing water and trap soil particles.

Terracing the slope is the ideal solution. When you remove the topsoil to create the terraces, set it aside and return it when the terraces are level. Provide a slight slope on each terrace along the contour line to prevent standing water. Retaining walls of wood or stone make the beds permanent. On heavy soils, lay lines of fired clay weep tiles or use gravel fill behind the walls to prevent bulging or collapse from water pressure.

If you just want to plant a few vegetables on sloping land and don't want to undertake a terracing project, try some of the watering ideas on page 46. Sunken, perforated milk cartons or other bottomless containers are particularly good for soaking hillside vegetables without water running downhill.

Ring of aluminum edging *lets water soak moisture loving squash instead of running downhill.*

Hillside gardener *uses both wood and stone to retain the soil on this terraced slope. Stone wall is covered with strawberries, gives extra depth to deep-rooted tomato plants in wire cylinders. Compost was added to all beds.*

Shopping for Seeds and Plants

Once you know which vegetables you want to grow, you must decide whether to start them from seeds or from purchased plants. When starting from seeds, you save money, have a wider selection of varieties to choose from, and enjoy the satisfaction of "starting from scratch."

A great many vegetables sprout quickly and grow easily from seeds planted in the ground, including beans, beets, carrots, cucumbers, corn, and radishes. But some vegetables sprout or grow slowly and mature late. These kinds (cabbage, eggplant, pepper, tomato, and some herbs) are easier to buy as plants or to start in containers. To find out the best way to start a specific vegetable, see the Gardener's Guide, pages 56-95.

Seed racks *allow you to choose and plant the same day.*

SEED BUYING TIPS

Before you buy any seeds, consider the pros and cons of both seed catalogs and display racks in stores. Most catalogs offer you a wider selection than store racks, but when you buy from a store, you can plant the seeds right away.

New varieties and hybrids are constantly being developed. In selecting your seeds, don't be so stubbornly loyal to the familiar kinds that you deprive yourself of the improvements plant breeders develop in new hybrids, particularly disease resistance. Well-known varieties aren't necessarily the best. A good example is 'Stringless Green Pod' bean, a variety that is about 100 years old. It is susceptible to a number of diseases caused by viruses, bacteria, and fungi and is only moderately productive. Yet gardeners continue to plant it, perhaps because of its familiar name.

Ready-made mixtures containing blends of several varieties of one vegetable offer an interesting way to try different varieties. For example, lettuce seed blends can give you an assortment of leaf colors and shapes for salads. Radish blends contain seeds of white, red, and red-white combinations. Sweet corn seed mixtures should be planted only when you have space for a sizable block because the differences in maturity dates can result in sparse pollination in small plots.

Seed racks

Seed racks in retail stores are a convenient source of better-known vegetable varieties, but they rarely offer unusual varieties or new hybrid seeds.

Displays usually contain the varieties that are known to perform dependably in your area. Yet they may include some popular but poorly adapted varieties. If you are in doubt about the varieties you have selected, ask a knowledgeable salesperson to review your choices before ringing up the sale.

Federal and state seed laws require the seeds you buy from racks to meet minimum germination standards. Racks of fresh seeds are usually put up in early spring and removed in late summer, except in California, Arizona, Florida, and Gulf Coast areas, where seeds are on sale year round and packages are replaced twice yearly.

Buy only what you can use in one season and check the seed packages for expiration dates. Many seeds, such as onions and parsnips, are short lived. Shop for seeds as soon as the fresh seed racks appear in the stores, because the first warm weekend brings a buying rush that will deplete the selection of varieties. Displays in larger stores, however, are frequently restocked.

Seed catalogs

Companies that sell vegetable seeds primarily through retail stores include Ferry Morse, Northrup King, Mandeville King, and Fredonia Seed Co. Following is a list of seed companies that specialize in mail order sales. Write to any of them for a catalog.

Burgess Seed and Plant Co., P.O. Box 218, Galesburg, Michigan 49053. All seeds are untreated.

W. Atlee Burpee. Write to the branch nearest you: Box 748, Riverside, Calif. 92502; Box 6929, Philadelphia, Pa. 19132; 615 North Second St., Clinton, Iowa 52732.

Farmer Seed and Nursery Co., Faribault, Minnesota 55021. Emphasis on early and cold resistant varieties suited to Northern states. Also a good selection of midget vegetables.

Henry Field Seed and Nursery Co., 407 Sycamore St., Shenandoah, Iowa 51602.

Gurney Seed and Nursery Co., 1448 Page St., Yankton, South Dakota 57078. Varieties suited to Northern climates. Many unusual vegetables.

Joseph Harris Co., Moreton Farm, Rochester, New York 14624. Emphasis on Northeastern states.

H. G. Hastings, P.O. Box 4088, Atlanta, Georgia 30302. Varieties for Southern states.

Jackson and Perkins, P.O. Box 217A, Medford, Oregon 97501.

J. W. Jung Seed Co., Randolph, Wisconsin 53956.

Earl May Seed and Nursery Co., Shenandoah, Iowa 51603.

Nichols Garden Nursery, 1190 North Pacific Highway, Albany, Oregon 97321. Wide selection of herbs and unusual vegetables.

George W. Park Seed Co., Greenwood, South Carolina 29647.

Seedway, Hall, New York 14463.

R. H. Shumway Seedsman, 628 Cedar St., Rockford, Illinois 61101.

Stokes Seeds Inc., Box 548 Main Post Office, Buffalo, New York 14240. Emphasis on vegetables that do well in Northern climates.

Wyatt-Quarles Seed Co., P.O. Box 2131, Raleigh, North Carolina 27602. Varieties adapted to the South.

Seed catalogs

A wider variety of seeds is offered in catalogs than on the display racks of retail stores. Many of the new "All-America Selections," as well as other improved hybrids, can be found only in catalogs.

Which catalog? Although some catalogs are nationally distributed, others are limited to a particular region. In catalogs distributed nationally, look for descriptions that assist you in choosing varieties or hybrids suited to your area. Be cautious about ordering from regional seed companies in distant states; if the climate of their region is widely different from yours, many of the varieties they offer may be unsuitable in your area. However, certain regional catalogs contain a rich assortment of facts about seeds and gardening. Many also offer proprietary hybrids that are available from no other source.

How to read catalogs. To make a rational selection when ordering seeds, look for answers to these questions when you read the catalogs:

• Does this variety or hybrid offer bred-in resistance to any common diseases?

• How early is the harvest of the variety or hybrid compared to others in the catalog? Look for the number of days to maturity, keeping in mind that these are based on ideal conditions. Early harvest is of the greatest value where summers are short. Late-maturing varieties usually yield more but require more warm days to ripen.

• Does this variety offer a greater yield than others?

• Is the taste mentioned? If not, the variety may have been developed for commercial gardening for which storage, shipping, or processing features are more important than good flavor.

• Does the variety carry an All-America award? This means that a vegetable performed much better than other home garden varieties and hybrids grown for comparison in about two dozen trial grounds.

• Does the description include the word "new"? Seeds of new varieties are often more expensive, but they are usually better in one or more ways than older ones. For example, they may offer greater disease resistance.

Special kinds of seeds

In seed racks and in catalogs, hybrids will be offered, as well as some of the more unusual vegetables. You'll see seed tapes and pelleted seeds, too—devices that simplify handling and spacing of seeds.

Hybrids. Hybrid sweet corn, developed in the 1920s, provides perhaps the best example of why hybrids are better than open-pollinated varieties. (Open-pollinated seeds come from seed fields in which cross-pollination is not controlled.) Though the old favorite 'Golden Bantam' requires about 80 days to mature, many hybrids are ready to eat in about 65 days, will sprout in cooler soil, and will bear much larger ears. Breeders have introduced genes for super sweetness, making new hybrids

Plant for compatibility

Gardeners have noticed for centuries that certain plants seem to grow better in the company of certain other plants. These can be plants whose roots don't compete for nutrients, whose foliage doesn't battle for light, or whose influence on soil chemistry is in each other's favor. Here are some combinations to try:

• Beans, corn, and squash or cucumbers
• Carrots and peas
• Tomatoes, chives, onions, and parsley
• Lettuce, carrots, and radishes
• Any of the legumes next to or in rotation with heavy nitrogen users

Experiments with strong-smelling plants that benefit other plants by discouraging pests have resulted in one definite conclusion: the roots of marigolds give off a chemical that repels nematodes within a three-foot radius of the plant. (The most common kind of nematodes produce nodules or swellings on plant roots.) That's as far as the scientific evidence goes, but some gardeners claim success with garlic plants repelling aphids and caterpillars.

---

so good that harvested ears can be eaten almost without cooking.

Hybrid tomatoes are another good example of hybrid superiority. The best performers are usually hybrids because of their large fruits, heavy yields, and more vigorous, disease-resistant plants. Hybrid kinds of cabbage, broccoli, carrots, onions, and spinach are superior to nonhybrids mostly in uniform maturity, yield, and size.

Vegetable curiosities. Garden magazine ads sometimes offer such oddities as vegetable spaghetti, white eggplant, yardlong beans, purple pod beans, purple head cauliflower, Italian eggplant, lemon cucumbers, and golden tomatoes. Some of the very strange-sounding novelties are delicious, but others can be disappointing. If you like to try different foods, plant one or two unusual vegetables each season, but also plant more conventional varieties in case you don't like the new tastes.

The midgets and giants of the vegetable world have their pros and cons. Midgets are generally small fruited and short lived. However, if your garden is small or if you want an early harvest, they are a sensible choice. Giants are usually quite late maturing and greedy for space. But if you are growing entries for a county fair or just to hear your neighbors exclaim, you should choose one of the mammoth varieties.

Pelleted seeds. Layers of fertilizer, fungicide, and inert material coat pelleted seeds to make them larger, more round, and easier to handle. Pelleted seeds are not widely distributed; you may find them in some seed displays. The packets are usually color coded to distinguish them from regular seeds.

Seed tapes. These are made by wrapping seeds in a thin, water-soluble plastic tape. The distance between seeds within the tape depends on how much room each vegetable needs. The seed tape is designed to be laid in a shallow furrow and covered with soil. Seed tapes are sold in spools 10 to 15 feet long. Descriptions and instructions are very simple for beginning gardeners, who can gain the most from the pre-spaced tapes.

BUYING VEGETABLE PLANTS

Although planting your own seeds is more economical and gives you a wider selection, buying seedling plants has some advantages. Seedling plants have a head start over seeds—important if your growing season is short. You also avoid the problems of germinating hard-to-sprout seeds.

Seedlings of some difficult-to-transplant vegetables are sold in peat pots. You can put these directly into the planting hole without disturbing the roots. The roots will grow through the walls of the pot. Since the peat pot becomes water repellent when it dries, keep the transplanted pot continually moist and cover the top edge completely with soil after planting so it has a chance to break down and become part of the soil.

Plant size. The size of plants you should buy depends on your budget and the amount of space you are planting. A beautiful, blooming tomato plant in a 4-inch pot is ideal for a single container, but if you have more space, a pack of six smaller tomato plants costs little more than one larger plant.

Plant condition. Look for plants that growers call "thrifty." Thrifty plants are compact, with full foliage and well-branched stems. Avoid tall, lanky plants. They have too much top in proportion to their root system and can suffer severe setbacks when transplanted. Yellowish green or discolored plants may have been poorly nourished or kept out of sunlight by the retailer. Purplish bronze coloration on cabbage, broccoli, or cauliflower plants generally indicates that they have been properly "hardened-off" or acclimatized and will adapt better to cold weather planting.

Caring for purchased plants. Water the plants and set them in a sunny corner of a porch, out of the wind. At night, cover them with a cardboard box to protect them against the cold. Gradual acclimatization for a couple of days before planting will help harden-off plants that otherwise might be shocked by a sudden transition from the warm greenhouse to the garden. During this time you should prepare your soil for transplanting (see page 21). This is a good time to prune off any lanky side branches to help young plants adapt more quickly to garden conditions when they are transplanted.

Peat pot *eliminates need to disturb roots when transplanting. Roots grow through pot's side.*

Water-soluble seed tape *contains correctly-spaced seeds. Lay tape in furrow, cut to size, and cover with soil.*

Soil is More than Dirt

You'll need to understand a few fundamentals about soil before you start to plant. In garden soil, air, water, solar energy, bacteria, fungi, humus (decaying organic material), and a host of small organisms (such as earthworms) interact with soil particles to produce a good environment, encouraging seeds to sprout and roots to grow. At the same time, many factors can disrupt this balance. Most soil problems stem from poor physical conditions. Compaction is the most troublesome. Soil compaction can restrict free entry of air, penetration and drainage of water, and activity of all soil organisms. Breaking up compacted soil is the first step in counteracting this condition; adding soil amendments keeps the soil from becoming compacted again. Before you

Bonemeal and rotted manure *add nutrients and loosen soil.*

prepare your soil for seeds and plants, you should try to identify the type of soil you have and learn how to improve it.

SOIL TYPES

There are roughly four different types of garden soil, based on differences in structure and texture: clay, sand and gravel, silt, and loam. A fifth type, organic soil, is less common around homesites. The descriptions that follow will help you identify your soil type.

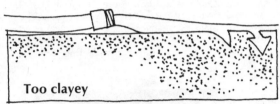

Too clayey

Tiny clay particles *inhibit root growth by preventing air and water from passing through the soil.*

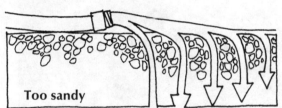

Too sandy

Large sand particles *let water drain too quickly. Soil needs more frequent watering and feeding than clay soil.*

Clay soils

Clay soil, composed of many small, flat particles, feels sticky or plastic in your hands. Clay comes in many colors: red, yellow, bluish gray, or almost black. Clay soils warm up and dry out slowly, take in water slowly, and can store reserves of nutrients better than most other soils.

Clay can become as hard as a rock during dry, warm weather if not watered regularly. Once dried out, it is almost impossible to water clay soil adequately with sprinklers. The surface seals over and stops water from penetrating easily. If this happens, you should make irrigation furrows to hold the water until it can soak in. Improve clay soils by digging in generous amounts of organic matter, such as peat moss, compost, or well-rotted manure, to improve drainage and aeration. Gypsum also helps improve the texture of clay, but does not add nutrients to the soil. Adding only sand to clay will not improve it; the soil will continue to form crusts and bake hard.

Sand and gravel soils

If your soil looks and feels like a sandbox or gravel pit, you have sandy or gravelly soil. Sandy soil is easy to work and warms up rapidly. However, it dries out quickly and then may blow around. In direct sun it can reflect enough heat to damage a vegetable crop. Fortunately, most sandy soils contain enough clay particles to make them reasonably responsive to fertilizers. Pure sand contains almost no nutrients and has little capacity to store moisture. However, most sandy soils have enough clay particles to hold some nutrients.

Gravelly soils are usually a mixture of gravel and sand, silt, or clay. Generally low in organic matter, they are also low in natural fertility. The best way to improve sandy or gravelly soil is to remove the larger pebbles and stones; then add coarse organic matter, such as peat moss, compost, or well-rotted manure. Clay added to sandy or gravelly soils will tend to collect in impervious layers instead of improving the soil.

Silt soils

Silt has an intermediate size between clay and sand. It consists of small, gritty particles that can pack down very hard. Silt ranges in color from gray to tan, yellow, and red. It's usually not very fertile. Silt topsoils are often found over dense layers of clay that slow or stop drainage.

Both the topsoil and these lower layers should be broken up and kept loose by adding copious amounts of peat moss, compost, well-rotted sawdust, or wood shavings. Adding organic matter will improve the structure and fertility of silt soils. Adding clay or sand will not improve silt.

Loam

Loam contains various proportions of clay, silt, sand, and organic matter. The proportions of each determine how easy the soil is to cultivate and how productive it is. Sandy loam with a fairly high content of organic matter is the easiest to cultivate, water, and weed. A loam that contains more than one-third clay acts almost like solid clay and needs lots of added organic matter to make it easy to manage.

Organic soils

Dark in color, organic soils are composed largely of peat moss or leaf mold. Your soil is not likely to be organic unless your house is built on an old lakebed, bog, or forest site. Organic soils are easy to work, weed, and water, but may warm up slowly because they retain moisture.

Since organic soils are usually high in nitrogen, they can benefit from fertilizers high in phosphate and potassium. Micronutrient deficiencies (of iron, copper,

Vegetables in raised beds

Planting beds raised above the soil level can help you overcome many obstacles to growing vegetables successfully. If your soil is hard, infertile, and drains poorly, raised beds allow you a fresh start with a light, rich soil mix (especially good for root crops). If gophers are a problem, you can line the bottom of the bed with 1-inch chicken wire to keep them out. Snails and slugs are often intimidated by the bed, and any pests that do get in are isolated and easier to control. Watering, weeding, and cultivating all require less stooping. Water only goes to the productive areas of the garden, keeping paths and your feet dry. As a bonus, the raised soil tends to warm up faster in the spring, resulting in earlier crops. If you cover the bed with clear plastic or panes of glass, you have a coldframe that is ideal for starting seeds or protecting tender plants.

The simplest raised bed uses 2 by 12-inch redwood boards reinforced at the corners. Stakes nailed midway on the boards and driven into the ground support the walls. Drainage holes filled with gravel at the bottom of the bed will eliminate standing water. A good width for the bed is 4 or 5 feet; the center of a wider bed would be hard to reach. The length can vary to fit the garden. If you build more than one bed, leave room for a wheelbarrow to pass between them.

Fill the bed with a rich, light soil mix—such as equal parts peat moss, compost, and topsoil. Soak the bed before planting so the soil will settle to about 2 or 3 inches below the top of the bed. If you wait to soak the soil until after planting, many plants will sink and need replanting. Replenish the nutrients by adding organic material, such as rotted manure, at replanting time.

Raised bed *covered with glass traps light and heat for early lettuce. Uncover the bed on warm days.*

Melons, bush beans, and carrots *thrive in the loose, well-drained soil that fills raised beds.*

Gopherproof raised bed *lined with aviary wire keeps out burrowers. Compost fills the inside.*

cobalt, zinc, and manganese) are common in this kind of soil, especially in the Southeast, but can be remedied by using special fertilizers containing the missing nutrients.

ACID AND ALKALINE SOILS

Acid soils are common in areas that get lots of rainfall. In chemists' terms, acid soils give a p^H reading of less than 7. (p^H measures the hydrogen ion concentration on a relative scale from 1 to 14: p^H 7 is neutral, pure water; any p^H less than 7 is acid; any p^H greater than 7 is alkaline.) The soil becomes progressively more acid as calcium and magnesium ions are removed and hydrogen ions replace them. This happens naturally by leaching, plant growth, and the weathering of some rocks. If the soil is excessively acid, valuable micronutrients become soluble and can leach away.

Alkaline soils are more common in arid regions. They give a p^H reading higher than 7. Soils turn more alkaline as calcium, manganese, and sodium ions accumulate and replace hydrogen ions. Natural causes of this include low rainfall, poor drainage, and native limestone deposits.

Often alkaline soils are also too salty. In extreme cases, heavy white or brown salt deposits are left on the soil surface by evaporating water. Salt problems are made worse when softened or brackish water is used for irrigation and when fertilizers with a high salt content, such as manure, are spread.

How can you tell if your soil is acid or alkaline? A quick and dependable method is to buy an inexpensive soil test kit (available at most garden supply stores or through mail order catalogs) and follow the easy directions.

The ideal vegetable garden soil should be slightly acid to neutral in reaction (p^H 6 to 7). Don't be alarmed if your test reading is slightly alkaline (p^H 7 to 8). You can grow excellent vegetables on slightly alkaline soil. With the more elaborate soil testing kits, you can test the soil for the presence of major nutrients. In some states you can consult the Agricultural Extension Division of your state university for information about other sources of soil testing services.

The soil should be thoroughly tested before you add any chemicals that can alter the soil p^H, such as lime, dolomite, marl, agricultural sulfur, or aluminum sulfate (alum). That way, you'll know the right material to add and how much is needed.

Correcting acid soils

Ground limestone is effective in counteracting acidity—the calcium in the limestone neutralizes acids. It's usually necessary to reapply limestone every two to three years, but don't add any lime unless your soil test reading is below p^H 5.5 to 6.

If you can find it, use dolomitic lime, which contains both calcium and magnesium. Avoid hydrated or burned lime; their caustic action can easily burn your skin, and they leach away rapidly.

Correcting alkaline soils

Because soils usually turn alkaline for more than one reason, you may have to do several things to correct the problem. To reduce alkalinity on well-drained land, flood the soil for 24 to 48 hours to wash excess mineral salts down below the root zone. Counterbalance any slight remaining alkalinity by feeding plants with an acid-type fertilizer. However, if moderate alkalinity remains after leaching, add substantial amounts of acidic amendments, such as peat moss, ground bark, or sawdust to the soil.

On poorly drained land where alkalinity is often most severe (p^H reading of more than 8.5), treatments are complex and costly. To avoid the problem entirely, garden in raised beds or containers filled with good garden soil brought in from another area. If you can't do that, improve the drainage by drilling holes down through impermeable layers to porous soil below. Add to the soil sulfur-bearing improvers, such as gypsum, soil sulfur, or aluminum sulfate, according to manufacturer's directions. Water deeply to leach out salts.

ENRICHING YOUR GARDEN SOIL

A good garden soil should 1) soak up water readily, yet drain fairly rapidly; 2) hold enough moisture for plants to grow; 3) remain loose and crumbly even in dry weather; 4) have ample space for air to circulate and roots to grow freely; 5) be easy to work; and 6) produce good crops with only occasional applications of fertilizer. These kinds of soil usually have a pleasant smell and are full of earthworms.

Most good garden soils aren't formed naturally; they are man-made. The way to make the best garden soil is to use ample amounts of organic amendments. Because these materials are constantly being broken down and used in the soil, you should replenish them each time you prepare the soil for planting. Compost and many commercial products are good organic amendments. (You can also replenish the soil by a process called green manuring.) When you add organic amendments, put them down in a 3 to 6-inch-deep layer on top of the soil and work them in to a depth of 9 to 12 inches.

Homemade compost

The purpose of composting is to turn the waste materials from your garden and kitchen into a rich, organic, soil-conditioning material. A compost pile does this efficiently by accelerating the natural processes that occur when dead leaves, grasses, and other materials

(Continued on page 24)

Compost in the making

Three bottomless boxes make compost machine.

To turn the compost pile, first lift off the top box and set it on the ground.

Move compost into first box with pitchfork to start new stack.

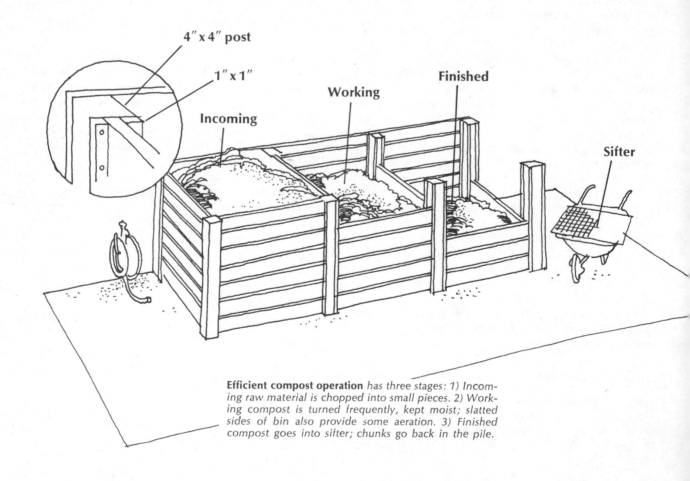

4" x 4" post

1" x 1"

Incoming

Working

Finished

Sifter

Efficient compost operation has three stages: 1) Incoming raw material is chopped into small pieces. 2) Working compost is turned frequently, kept moist; slatted sides of bin also provide some aeration. 3) Finished compost goes into sifter; chunks go back in the pile.

Set the emptied *second box of compost on top of the first box.*

Remaining compost *goes from the bottom of the old stack to the top of the new stack.*

Last box *goes on new stack, screens go on top.*

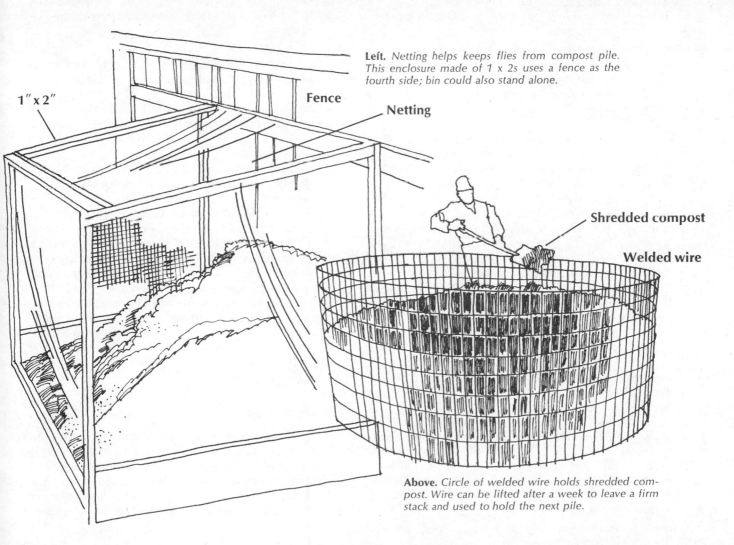

1" x 2"

Fence

Netting

Left. *Netting helps keeps flies from compost pile. This enclosure made of 1 x 2s uses a fence as the fourth side; bin could also stand alone.*

Shredded compost

Welded wire

Above. *Circle of welded wire holds shredded compost. Wire can be lifted after a week to leave a firm stack and used to hold the next pile.*

Compost grinder *turned prunings on left into pile on right, just the right size for the compost pile. This method is expensive but fast.*

Machete *makes less expensive but slower chopping tool than grinder.*

(Continued from page 21)
decompose. Piling organic materials up while they decay is better than digging them into the ground because, when piled up, they don't temporarily rob growing plants of available nitrogen while breaking down.

What you put in your compost pile will depend on the waste material available from your garden and kitchen, but you should follow a few basic rules so you don't create a trash pile.

1) Spread a layer of plant material, such as fallen leaves, green or dry weeds, and grass clippings, on a flat piece of cleared ground. Add layers of manure (or a few handfuls of a nitrogen-rich fertilizer), topsoil, and kitchen scraps (except meat, fat, and bones). Keep adding more layers until you've used up all the debris. Don't put too much of one material in the same layer or it will tend to pack together, slowing the breakdown and causing odor.

2) Chop or grind materials into small pieces before you add them to the pile. Smaller particles offer more surfaces for decay organisms to work on. Materials such as grass clippings that are too fine, however, should be mixed with coarser pieces so they don't turn into a slimy mass.

3) Heat build-up is essential to make compost. Too shallow a pile won't hold enough heat in, and breakdown will be slower. A compost pile 4 to 6 feet high will hold heat well and let air circulate. Some kind of a bin will make it easier to stack compost to this height. Steam rising from the pile is a sign that heat is being generated.

4) Keep the pile moist, but not soggy. Too much water limits the air supply. A pile with a slightly concave shape will catch and hold the moisture better. During prolonged periods of heavy rainfall, cover the pile with a plastic sheet or tarp to keep it from becoming soggy. If it does get too wet, frequent turning will restore it to a healthy condition.

5) Turn the pile every few weeks. Good air circulation discourages odor and flies and speeds decay. Turning also moves the outer, undecomposed material into the center so it can break down. Plenty of succulent material, such as lawn clippings and soft green weeds, should be well mixed with dry or woody materials.

6) Nitrogen is needed by the decay-producing bacteria. Sources of nitrogen are fresh manure, blood meal, sewage sludge, and commercial fertilizers.

7) Compost is ready to use when it is crumbly and the original materials have decomposed beyond recognition—usually about three months after the heap is built. Sift the compost before you use it to eliminate large, undecomposed chunks.

Green manure

Planting a green manure cover crop is a good way to add organic matter to your soil in a large garden. It is not, as its name suggests, a green-colored manure but a crop that is grown specifically for turning under. Any of the fast-growing members of the grass family (annual rye grass, barley, or oats) or the legume family (clover,

Tools you will need

You can prepare a planting bed and tend your vegetables with the basic tools that have been used for centuries: a shovel, rake, hoe, hand trowel, and weeding tool. You'll see a wide range of styles and prices, but look for well-built tools that fit your hands. For preparing beds, a round-pointed shovel will take care of most of the digging and amendment-moving jobs. A good, all-purpose hoe is the chopper type, which will work for making furrows and pulling the soil over planted seed, as well as for weeding.

If you make compost, you'll need a spading fork to turn the pile. A machete will come in handy, too, for chopping heavy stalks into small bits before you compost them. In areas where the soil is hard, you may need a pickax to break it up.

A wheel cultivator can take the place of some of these tools and is useful in a large vegetable garden that is planted in rows. Attachments serve to cut weed roots, loosen the soil, and form furrows, although the soil must be loosened initially by spading or a rototiller.

For very large gardens, power equipment, such as a rototiller for breaking up earth or a shredder-grinder for making compost, can save a great deal of work. You may want to rent, rather than buy, expensive equipment that you use infrequently. Renting before you buy will also help you decide whether to make the investment.

You're working a lot harder than you have to if you're not sharpening the tools that you use. The photos below show two ways of keeping them sharp: an electric grinding wheel and a flat hand file.

High-wheel *cultivator revived from turn of century makes a useful tool for weeding, making furrows.*

Sharpened spade *saves you work. Electric grinding wheel does the job fast. Let metal cool frequently.*

Sharpen hoe *on its back side with a flat, medium-coarse file, stroking in one direction only.*

vetch, lespedeza, broad beans, or peas) may be planted. You could also use mustard, kale, or other broad-leafed plants. Lawn grass seeds, such as bluegrass or fescue, grow too slowly to be practical.

A green manure crop is usually planted in early fall so that it will be half-grown by spring. The entire crop is then tilled into the ground a month or so before planting time. In regions with sub-zero winter temperatures, it's best to seed the crop between standing vegetables in late summer so plants can root before a heavy frost.

If you must delay turning the crop under because the soil is too wet, keep the crop down to an easily handled size by cutting it with a scythe, shears, or rotary mower. The crop does not have to be mature to be turned under. Although the top growth may be sparse, the well developed root system will add a substantial amount of organic matter as it decays.

Purchased organic amendments

If you want to save money, shop around for good, inexpensive, weed-free amendments or for amendments that are free for the hauling. Depending on where you live, you might find free peanut, rice, or almond hulls; pecan shells; cannery waste; cider mill pomace; or well-aged sludge from sewage treatment plants. (Cotton-producing states enforce regulations against the use of cotton gin wastes to prevent the spread of insects.)

Other amendments include the following:

Peat moss. This is a fairly expensive but excellent soil amendment. Several types are sold. Coarse brown sphagnum or hypnum peat moss is generally superior to sedge peats, which are usually black and extremely fine textured. Most peat moss sold in bales is air-dried. Wet it thoroughly before you mix it into the soil.

Wood products. Various wood products, mainly sawdusts and barks, are inexpensive substitutes for peat moss. These amendments are sold in bagged, baled, or bulk form (bulk form is the cheapest). You can get these products from commercial firms and sometimes directly from lumber mills or yards.

You can buy wood products either raw or treated. Raw sawdusts rob nitrogen from the soil as they break down, and a few kinds contain materials that can harm some types of plants. For that reason, most commercial products have been treated with nitrogen and allowed to compost to some degree before they are sold. These commercial wood products are generally safe to use for all kinds of plants. If you buy raw sawdust, add a nitrogen fertilizer to it and let it compost for a while before you dig it into the soil.

Manure

All forms of manure make useful soil amendments. They improve soil structure and act as mild fertilizers. Besides the manures mentioned below, other kinds, such as rabbit and sheep manure, may be available in some areas. These should be composted before using. In some arid regions where salt buildup in the soil is a problem, it's probably best to use soil conditioners other than manure.

Steer manure. Processed manures usually come from cattle feed lots. They've been treated to kill weed seeds. Use them sparingly (add no more than 8 cubic feet per 100 cubic feet of soil) as soil conditioners. Some kinds

Radishes grew best in balanced soil mix.

Ground bark conditioned soil but didn't have enough nutrients for good growth.

Manure acted as both a fertilizer and a soil conditioner to grow better radishes.

have high contents of soluble salts. Water heavily after sowing seeds or transplanting plants to wash away excess salts.

Fresh manure or stable litter. Fresh manure needs to be aged before it is used as a soil amendment or it will burn plants. Composting is a good way to age it. If the temperature remains high enough, many weed seeds that are usually present will be killed. (See composting, page 21.)

Fresh horse manure can also be dug into the soil to heat old-fashioned hotbeds (see page 31).

Poultry manure. Full of nutrients and virtually free of weed seeds, chicken or turkey manure has long been a favored soil amendment. It must be aged or composted before you mix it into the soil. Fresh poultry manure will quickly burn a newly-planted crop. Some gardeners use fresh chicken manure when they plant a green manure crop (see page 24) in the fall. The growing crop absorbs nutrients from the manure. After being spaded under the following spring, the decomposing material gradually and safely dispenses nutrients to the growing vegetables.

Sprouts from your kitchen

Neither insects nor the weather can affect the sprouts you grow in your kitchen, and you'll be eating the results within days instead of weeks or months.

There are two types of sprouts. The tiny ones that you eat when they form green leaves are alfalfa, cress, chia, mustard, and radish. The larger ones that you eat before the leaves open or turn green are fenugreek, lentils, mung beans (the kind you see in the grocery store), wheat, and rye. You use the same method to sprout both kinds.

First, soak the seeds in water until they are saturated —a few hours for the small ones, overnight for the large ones. Use a container that drains easily (such as a colan-der) for the larger sprouts; sprinkle smaller sprouts on damp cheesecloth spread in the bottom of a shallow dish (not metal). A glass jar with cheesecloth or screen fitted under the jar ring works well, too. Keep it on its side in filtered light.

Rinse or spray the seeds with lukewarm water several times a day. The object is to keep them moist (but not wet) and fairly warm (at least 68°).

When the seeds sprout, give them plenty of light, except for mung beans and fenugreek, which should be kept in the dark until ready for use. Use sprouts in cooked dishes, sandwiches, or salads with or without the seed hulls.

Scatter seeds thickly *over wet cheesecloth. Sprinkle with water.*

Fifth day *brings ready-to-eat sprouts about two inches tall.*

Give sprouted seeds *some light (but not full sun) and keep them moist.*

Starting Seeds and Transplants

The kinds of vegetables you want to grow and the climate of your area determine how you should plant— by starting seeds indoors, by sowing seeds directly in the ground, or by buying and setting out transplants. See the Planting Chart on pages 40-43 and the Gardener's Guide, pages 56-95, for the best way to start specific vegetables.

Start seeds indoors if they are difficult to sprout outdoors or if you want to get a head start on the growing season. Sow seeds in the ground of those vegetables that sprout easily and of those that are difficult to transplant. Buy plants if you are only growing a few or if avoiding the trouble of starting from seeds is worth the extra expense to you. Knowing how seeds sprout will

Transplant tomato plants *to roomier pots at this stage.*

help you decide on the best method.

All seeds are embryonic plants enclosed with a food reserve by a water-permeable coat. A seed germinates when heat, water, oxygen, and, sometimes, light create the right conditions.

Some seeds will rot if planted when the soil temperature is less than 65° to 70°; others will sprout and grow reliably at soil temperatures as low as 50°.

When seeds fail to germinate, the cause in most cases is lack of heat (cold soil) or too much water (poor drainage). In dry areas, the prime cause is often lack of water. Dryness can result in soil crusting, which restricts the entry of oxygen and water to the soil. Pathogenic soil fungi and bacteria can attack and kill seeds or sprouts, but they seldom cause a problem when soil temperature, moisture, and aeration are right.

GIVING SEEDS A HEAD START

You can control the heat and moisture levels more easily indoors or under cover outdoors to provide seeds with the optimum conditions they need for sprouting. (Optimum sprouting temperatures are listed on pages 40-43.) This is particularly important for slow-to-sprout seeds, but in areas with short, cool summers, even fast-growing vegetables, such as sweet corn and bush beans, will benefit if started indoors in plantable peat pots.

Materials you will need

The basic needs for starting most kinds of seeds indoors are few:
- Sterilized potting soil
- Milled sphagnum moss, vermiculite, or perlite

- Containers with drainage holes in the bottoms, such as flat, shallow aluminum foil pans, or plastic trays
- Small peat pots (2½-3-inch diameters)

Mail order firms also sell many kinds of devices to make seed starting easier. These include miniature greenhouses, compressed peat moss cylinders that expand when soaked in water, and preplanted kits.

Damping off diseases that kill seedlings as they sprout or shortly afterward can be a serious problem. Avoid this difficulty by sprouting seeds in a sterile medium, such as vermiculite, perlite, milled sphagnum moss, or a sterilized commercial planting mixture.

Vermiculite and perlite tend to retain moisture and are best used as a covering for seeds to keep them from drying out. Sphagnum moss (not the same as sphagnum peat moss) is best used as the actual growing medium because it contains a natural inhibitor that discourages the growth of bacteria and fungi. If you can't buy or mail order bags of sphagnum moss in the milled or pulverized form, you can grind up the rope-like "green moss."

Sphagnum moss often comes dried and must be thoroughly moistened before use. The easiest method is to place a quart of moss in a plastic bag and add a cup or two of water. Squeeze the bag to make the moss accept water and knead it until the moisture is evenly distributed.

How to plant seeds indoors

Fill seed-starting flats or pans with moistened moss or sterilized potting soil ½ inch from the top and firm it level. Scatter the seeds thinly and cover lightly with moistened moss, perlite, or vermiculite. Sprinkle the

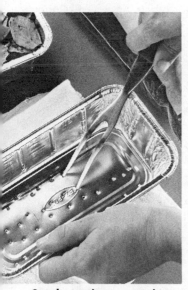

Seed-starting container *must have drainage, ample depth for roots.*

Scatter seeds *evenly on top of lightweight commercial or homemade potting soil; don't let the soil dry out.*

Vermiculite *holds moisture in to help seeds germinate. See that soil gets watered too, not just the vermiculite.*

Starting your seeds early

Above. Plastic bag covers pot holding sprouted seeds. The plastic keeps moisture in, insuring germination.

Near left. Paper cups with holes punched for drainage make good seed-starting containers. Tear cup away from rootball to plant.

Left. After watered peat pellet expands into a "pot," plant seed in it; later, when seedling is up, plant the whole thing.

seeds lightly each day until they sprout. If you cover the pan with plastic film after a thorough moistening, you won't have to water again until the seeds sprout. Keep the pan out of direct sunlight. When the first sprouts appear, remove the film and set the pan beside a sunny window. If nights become very cold, however, move the containers away from the glass.

When the second pair of leaves opens, it's time to transplant the seedlings. After they have adjusted to larger containers by showing new growth, you can begin to expose them to outdoor temperatures when it's sunny and nights are mild.

Sowing seeds directly in peat pots prevents giving small seedlings a transplant shock. Cucumbers, squash, and melons are particularly set back by transplanting; this defeats the purpose of giving them an early start. The peat pot allows you to place the entire plant and pot into the soil as soon as the roots penetrate the containers. Start such large, fast-sprouting seeds in peat pots only three to four weeks before outdoor planting time. Before setting the plants in peat pots out in the garden, thoroughly soak the pots until they are dark brown and soft. If they are set into the earth while dry, it is hard to soak them by watering, and the roots cannot penetrate the pot walls.

Time your planting

Be wary of starting your seeds too early, a common problem in starting them indoors. Ordinarily, 8 to 12 weeks before the average date of the last killing frost in the spring is soon enough. Seeds planted too early have to cope with short, gloomy days, frigid nights, and extremely dry air inside heated homes. And if you are successful in sprouting and growing a number of varieties, you're faced with the problem of what to do with dozens of plants if it's too cold to set them outside. With proper timing, started plants can be transplanted into peat pots and set out for two to three weeks prior to the frost-free date. Check the Planting Chart, pages 40-43, for the best time to plant each vegetable indoors.

Simulating a greenhouse

A greenhouse, of course, would be the ideal location for starting seeds. But if you are not starting vast amounts of seeds, you can create greenhouse conditions in other, less elaborate, ways. Starting seeds indoors provides room temperature warmth; covering the container with plastic film maintains moisture for sprouting. Some seeds sprout better with added warmth; those begun outdoors need protection from cold and from drying out that a cover provides.

Artificial light. Since all seeds are covered with some soil at planting, light from the sun or from fluorescent lamps serves mostly to provide heat. Light becomes necessary for photosynthesis and growth as soon as the first sprout shows above the soil.

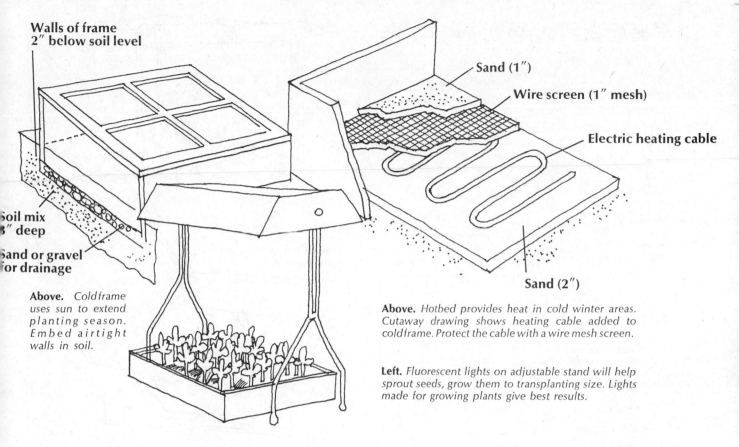

**Walls of frame
2″ below soil level**

Sand (1″)

Wire screen (1″ mesh)

Electric heating cable

Soil mix
3″ deep

Sand or gravel
for drainage

Sand (2″)

Above. *Coldframe uses sun to extend planting season. Embed airtight walls in soil.*

Above. *Hotbed provides heat in cold winter areas. Cutaway drawing shows heating cable added to coldframe. Protect the cable with a wire mesh screen.*

Left. *Fluorescent lights on adjustable stand will help sprout seeds, grow them to transplanting size. Lights made for growing plants give best results.*

Fluorescent lamps above the plant can provide both heat for sprouting seeds and light to grow seedlings. Certain kinds of fluorescent lamps are especially made for growing plants; these lamps concentrate more energy in the red, far red, and blue areas of the spectrum. They are more expensive than ordinary fluorescent lamps, but they hasten seed germination and seedling growth.

In sprouting seeds, use the gentle warmth and radiant energy from the tubes by positioning seed pans only 3 or 4 inches below the tubes. Burn the tubes constantly until the sprouts have emerged; then give the young sprouts 12 to 16 hours of light daily.

Once seeds have sprouted, they will grow into compact seedlings under temperatures of 60 to 65°. After the seeds have sprouted, place the seedlings no more than 12 inches below the tubes. At greater distances from the light source, light intensity falls off drastically, causing seedlings to become leggy.

Coldframes. A coldframe is a low-profile structure with a slanting, transparent roof that provides a protected area for early spring and late-fall growing. Simple to construct, these devices are useful during most of the year. Coldframes capture solar heat during the day and hold some of it through the night, protecting seedlings against frost damage. Since the coldframe is heated by the sun, slant it toward the south and paint the interior white to reflect more sunlight onto the plants. When

temperatures drop below 32°, the frame should be covered with a tarp or plastic film. On warm days, cool the bed by raising the sash.

Cover the floor of the coldframe with fast-draining sand. A light potting mix on top of this should be 3 inches deep for sowing seed. If you sow seed in flats, raise the flats off the floor by setting them on blocks.

Hotbeds. When you bury electric cables in the floor of a coldframe, you have a hotbed that is especially useful for hard-to-germinate seeds. (Use heating cables made for this purpose.) Incandescent bulbs are not as good as a heat source because they have little effect on soil temperature. Fresh manure dug into the soil beneath a coldframe is another method of providing heat.

When electric cables are used to heat hotbeds, you can sow seeds in the soil directly above them; in fact, some gardeners grow winter crops of vegetables this way. Most gardeners, however, use hotbeds first for sprouting seeds and later, without heat, as coldframes for growing seedlings to the size for transplanting to the garden. Cover floors of hotbeds with fast-draining fine gravel or sand, providing a clean area for placing flats and pots and for evaporating moisture to raise the humidity.

Where winters are severe, pile up earth around hotbeds to give more insulation. Covers made of two layers of glass or plastic with an air space between will decrease loss of heat by radiation.

Covering outdoor seedbeds

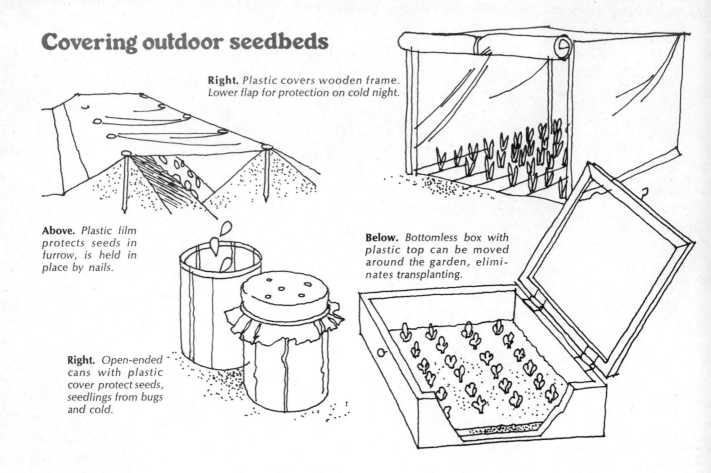

Right. *Plastic covers wooden frame. Lower flap for protection on cold night.*

Above. *Plastic film protects seeds in furrow, is held in place by nails.*

Below. *Bottomless box with plastic top can be moved around the garden, eliminates transplanting.*

Right. *Open-ended cans with plastic cover protect seeds, seedlings from bugs and cold.*

Covered seedbeds. A number of useful devices are based on the principle of the coldframe. European gardeners have long used cloches, interlocking A-frame glass canopies (with closed ends) over rows of seedlings (mainly frost-tender leafy types) to add growing time to both ends of the season, and to protect warmth-loving vegetables. Most cloches are held in wire carrying frames and can be taken apart for storage. Modern cloches employ sheet plastic over wire hoops. Bury the edges of the plastic in the soil. Open both ends of the shelter on warm days to prevent vegetables from literally becoming cooked.

Individual, heavy, waxed paper bonnets can be placed over individual seedlings. The caps trap solar heat and speed growth, as well as protect plants from frost damage. No covering can protect against extreme cold, though, so don't set warmth-loving plants in the garden until all heavy frosts are past.

SOWING SEEDS IN THE GROUND

Planting seeds in the ground without protection gives you less control over the factors that affect germination than with seeds started indoors. But, when seeds fail to sprout, it's probably the result of one of these conditions:

- Seeds may rot because the soil is too cold (too early planting).
- Seeds planted too deep may not reach soil surface.
- Seeds may be unable to break through crusts on dried-out soil surface.
- Seeds may lack enough moisture to sprout when the soil is allowed to dry out.

You can control these problems by timing the planting correctly, by preparing the seedbed properly and keeping it watered, and by sowing each type of seed at the right depth.

Preparing the seedbed

Seeds sprout best in a moist, well-drained, well-pulverized soil. You can work up the soil either several weeks or a few days before planting. To an often-used garden soil, simply add a fresh supply of amendments and work them in. You will have to use more elaborate techniques to prepare soil that has never been gardened before.

Soil preparation. To establish a new vegetable garden in an old lawn or weed patch:

- Remove all debris and strip the plot of any sod—the top layer of soil containing the roots of grass or weeds.

• Stack the sod to the side, upside down. Scatter a high nitrogen fertilizer between each layer of sod and water the pile occasionally to hasten decomposition. (Water the stack occasionally to turn it into compost you can use the next time you prepare the soil.)
• Spade or till the soil thoroughly until it is well pulverized.
• Spread a 2 to 3-inch layer of soil amendment and any additional fertilizer at the rate recommended on the package. Work these into the soil.

Forming beds and furrows. After you have spaded the soil and incorporated amendments, form beds for planting. Use the conventional method described here or the French intensive method described on page 35.

Every three feet, dig a furrow to spade depth and use the excavated soil to build up beds on either side. The furrows between beds serve, in dry climates, to pond irrigation water or, where rainfall is heavy, to drain-off the excess. Level the beds; then rake lightly to skim off pebbles.

Timing the planting

When you plant depends on the weather and the crops you are planting. Generally, seeds of leafy vegetables won't rot if planted too early; neither will most root crops or pea seeds. But seeds of beans, corn, cucumbers, squash, melon, okra, Southern peas, and other heat-loving crops will rot if planted in cold soil.

Consult the chart (below) for average dates of the last frosts in the spring and the first in the fall; plant frost-tender vegetables so that they will mature between these dates. You can also purchase an inexpensive soil thermometer and follow the Planting Chart on page 40, which gives the optimum soil temperature for sprouting seeds of each kind. (Soil temperature generally lags 10 days to 2 weeks behind air temperature.)

(Continued on page 34)

Average Hard-Frost Dates*

Based on U.S.D.A. weather records

State	Last in Spring	First in Fall	State	Last in Spring	First in Fall	State	Last in Spring	First in Fall
Alabama, N.W.	Mar. 25	Oct. 30	Kentucky	Apr. 15	Oct. 20	N. Dakota, E.	May 16	Sept. 20
Alabama, S.E.	Mar. 8	Nov. 15	Louisiana, No.	Mar. 13	Nov. 10	Ohio, No.	May 6	Oct. 15
Arizona, No.	Apr. 23	Oct. 19	Louisiana, So.	Feb. 20	Nov. 20	Ohio, So.	Apr. 20	Oct. 20
Arizona, So.	Mar. 1	Dec. 1	Maine	May 25	Sept. 25	Oklahoma	Apr. 2	Nov. 2
Arkansas, No.	Apr. 7	Oct. 23	Maryland	Apr. 19	Oct. 20	Oregon, W.	Apr. 17	Oct. 25
Arkansas, So.	Mar. 25	Nov. 3	Massachusetts	Apr. 25	Oct. 25	Oregon, E.	June 4	Sept. 22
California			Michigan, Upper pen.	May 25	Sept. 15	Pennsylvania, W.	Apr. 20	Oct. 10
Imperial Valley	Jan. 25	Dec. 15	Michigan, No.	May 17	Sept. 25	Pennsylvania, Cen.	May 1	Oct. 15
Interior Valley	Mar. 1	Nov. 15	Michigan, So.	May 10	Oct. 8	Pennsylvania, E.	Apr. 17	Oct. 15
Southern Coast	Jan. 15	Dec. 15	Minnesota, No.	May 25	Sept. 15	Rhode Island	Apr. 25	Oct. 25
Central Coast	Feb. 25	Dec. 1	Minnesota, So.	May 11	Oct. 1	S. Carolina, N.W.	Apr. 1	Nov. 8
Mountain Sections	Apr. 25	Sept. 1	Mississippi, No.	Mar. 25	Oct. 30	S. Carolina, S.E.	Mar. 15	Nov. 15
Colorado, West	May 25	Sept. 18	Mississippi, So.	Mar. 15	Nov. 15	S. Dakota	May 15	Sept. 25
Colorado, N.E.	May 11	Sept. 27	Missouri	Apr. 20	Oct. 20	Tennessee	Apr. 10	Oct. 25
Colorado, S.E.	May 1	Oct. 15	Montana	May 21	Sept. 22	Texas, N.W.	Apr. 15	Nov. 1
Connecticut	Apr. 25	Oct. 20	Nebraska, W.	May 11	Oct. 4	Texas, N.E.	Mar. 21	Nov. 10
Delaware	Apr. 15	Oct. 25	Nebraska, E.	Apr. 15	Oct. 15	Texas, So.	Feb. 10	Dec. 15
District of Columbia	Apr. 11	Oct. 23	Nevada, W.	May 19	Sept. 22	Utah	Apr. 26	Oct. 19
Florida, No.	Feb. 25	Dec. 5	Nevada, E.	June 1	Sept. 14	Vermont	May 23	Sept. 25
Florida, Cen.	Feb. 11	Dec. 28	New Hampshire	May 23	Sept. 25	Virginia, No.	Apr. 15	Oct. 25
Florida, South of Lake Okeechobee, almost frost-free			New Jersey	Apr. 20	Oct. 25	Virginia, So.	Apr. 10	Oct. 30
Georgia, No.	Apr. 1	Nov. 1	New Mexico, No.	Apr. 23	Oct. 17	Washington, W.	Apr. 10	Nov. 15
Georgia, So.	Mar. 15	Nov. 15	New Mexico, So.	Apr. 1	Nov. 1	Washington, E.	May 15	Oct. 1
Idaho	May 21	Sept. 22	New York, W.	May 10	Oct. 8	W. Virginia, W.	May 1	Oct. 15
Illinois, No.	May 1	Oct. 8	New York, E.	May 1	Oct. 15	W. Virginia, E.	May 15	Oct. 1
Illinois, So.	Apr. 15	Oct. 20	New York, No.	May 15	Oct. 1	Wisconsin, No.	May 17	Sept. 25
Indiana, No.	May 1	Oct. 8	N. Carolina, W.	Apr. 15	Oct. 25	Wisconsin, So.	May 1	Oct. 10
Indiana, So.	Apr. 15	Oct. 20	N. Carolina, E.	Apr. 8	Nov. 1	Wyoming, W.	June 20	Aug. 20
Iowa, No.	May 1	Oct. 2	N. Dakota, W.	May 21	Sept. 13	Wyoming, E.	May 21	Sept. 20
Iowa, So.	Apr. 15	Oct. 9						
Kansas	Apr. 20	Oct. 15						

*Allow 10 days either side of above dates to meet local conditions and seasonal differences.

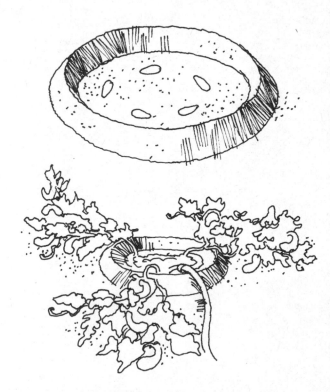

Apply bands of fertilizer parallel to seed furrows. Nutrients reach roots when plants are ready for them.

Make furrows at planting time for large vegetables that will need deep soaking. Enlarge as needed.

Sowing the seeds

Most gardeners plant in straight rows to help them distinguish the seedlings from the weeds. Planting in 4 to 6-inch bands on raised mounds, though, is a sure way of getting greater yields of the small vegetables from a given area. This method requires a high level of soil fertility and more frequent watering. Planting in masses also requires hand weeding, since a hoe is only practical between rows.

Mark rows or bands with the date planted and the name of the variety. Use a plastic lettering device or weatherproof plastic markers with lettering that won't wash away.

Furrows. To plant seeds in a row, make a long, shallow ditch with the corner of a hoe. Stretch twine taut between pegs at the ends of the row to make furrows straight. Form furrows for small seeds by pressing the edge of a board into cultivated soil to make a "vee." After sowing seeds in rows, cover them with soil.

Hill planting. Large vegetables, such as corn, squash, and beans, are sometimes planted in "hills." This is a cluster of seeds—not necessarily on a raised mound. The object is for the roots to range out from the central growing point to get more foraging room in the soil. Plant five to eight seeds in a 12 to 18-inch circle and thin to three plants (see illustrations below).

Planting depth. To gauge the proper planting depth, follow the old rule of thumb, planting a seed to a depth

Hill planting means a circle of seeds (above). Watering basin keeps water off the vines.

French intensive method

This Gallic technique can produce a maximum harvest and superior vegetables from your garden space, but it demands a lot of digging. Based on the method used centuries ago by French farmers who had abundant supplies of manure and heavy, shallow soils, French intensive gardening relies on closely spaced planting in deeply dug and richly amended beds. The organic material worked into the soil before planting breaks up hard soil and supplies enough nutrients so you won't have to fertilize throughout the growing season. Raised beds provide aeration and good drainage. The close spacing reduces weeds, moisture loss, and soil crusting and also helps maintain an even soil temperature.

When you've finished digging, let the bed sit for a couple of days. Then break up clods and work the soil to a fine texture. Sprinkle a dusting of bone meal, an inch of rotted manure, and some wood ashes over the bed. Turn these materials into the top 3 to 6 inches, rake the mound smooth, and soak the soil with a gentle spray.

Whether you set out transplants or sow seeds, the spacing object is to set plants at intervals so the outer leaves will just touch as they approach mature size. This is easier to judge with transplants than with seeds, but you can always thin and use plants from a thick seeding.

The close spacing is more practical for the leaf and root crops, such as lettuce, spinach, cabbage, beets, carrots, and turnips. You can use the raised beds for larger vegetables, but plant them in rows with the usual spacing.

Closely-spaced turnips, planted in staggered lines, are thinned as they grow. Cook the thinnings.

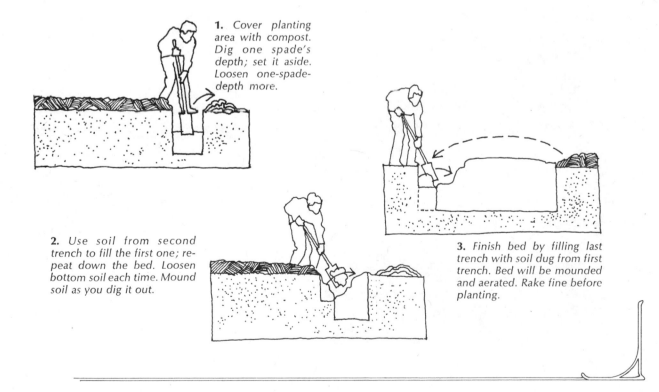

1. Cover planting area with compost. Dig one spade's depth; set it aside. Loosen one-spade-depth more.

2. Use soil from second trench to fill the first one; repeat down the bed. Loosen bottom soil each time. Mound soil as you dig it out.

3. Finish bed by filling last trench with soil dug from first trench. Bed will be mounded and aerated. Rake fine before planting.

not more than three times its size. Check the Planting Chart on pages 40-43 and read instructions on seed packets for exact planting depths. If you plant seeds too deep, they may germinate but perish before making it to the surface. (Small seeds have only a limited store of carbohydrates to sustain them while their sprouts are forcing their way upward to the sunlight.)

The only time to alter the planting depth rule is in the heat of summer when the soil dries out quickly. If you cover the seeds with a non-crusting mulch, you can plant them at twice the usual depth.

Watering the seedbed

You will have to water often enough to keep the soil moist for sprouting seeds if the normal rainfall doesn't do it for you. Morning and evening sprinkling will keep the soil moist enough for sprouting. A perforated plastic sprinkler hose is good for this task because it makes small droplets that don't wash soil away. Water long enough to wet the soil to about a 6-inch depth. If you don't have a sprinkler, you can use a fine mist spray from a hose nozzle.

If you live in a dry climate, you can imitate the commercial growers, who pond water in furrows for an hour or so. Since water does not move very far in a horizontal direction, you will have to place rows of seeds near the shoulders of the bed to achieve adequate wetting. Watch the moisture as it soaks laterally into the bed; when it has wet the soil a few inches beyond the row, move the hose to another furrow. Dig these furrows at planting time.

Out of room? Hang it up

Cherry tomatoes, cucumbers, eggplant, and New Zealand spinach make prime candidates for a dramatic and productive hanging basket on the patio. Choose a clay pot or wooden box with holes in the rim or line a wire basket with moss and then fill with soil. (A 12-inch container is a good size for most vegetables.) Since the container will be very heavy when wet and loaded with mature plants, use big hooks for hanging them and double up on the wire supports.

Follow instructions for planting containers (page 7). When you hang the basket, check that the bottom is high enough to avoid heads (about 7 feet).

Plant in 4-inch-square peat pot goes into 12-inch clay pot. Peat pot was soaked and surrounded with loose soil.

Hanging cherry tomato graces patio, provides snacks for passers-by. Plant needs full sun and frequent watering.

Preventing soil crusts. Crusts often form in clay or silt soils, seal out air and moisture, and physically resist penetration by sprouts. Germination can be improved by covering seeds with a granular material, such as vermiculite, perlite, or sand. After soaking the soil and sowing the seeds, cover them to a depth equal to two to three times their size; then firm the covering. Water the rows lightly daily until the seeds have sprouted. (Use a light spray to keep the seedbeds moist; a heavy spray can wash tiny seeds and seedlings away.)

Keeping the soil moist. During dry spells you may have to resort to covering seedbeds with plastic sheeting or burlap kept moist by frequent sprinkling, especially for such slow-sprouting seeds as parsley.

One of the best devices for improving dry-weather germination is a wide board laid over a deep furrow. Soak the furrow, scatter the seeds thinly, and cover them very lightly with soil. Lay the board over the furrow. Remove it occasionally for watering the seeds and to inspect for spots of mold. If you see any gray mold, remove the board temporarily so that sunlight can kill the disease. Remove the board as soon as seeds begin to sprout.

Thinning seedlings

Try to sow seeds the recommended distance apart given on the seed packages and in the Planting Chart on pages 40-43. With small seeds, pour a few from the packet into your palm and take small pinches. With a little manipulation, you can drop seeds the required distance apart in the furrow. (Using seed tapes or pelleted seeds for small or expensive seeds eliminates waste.) Thin seeding is also healthy for the seedlings that sprout. Thickly seeded plants can grow together so closely you can injure the roots of the survivors when you thin out excess plants.

Any crowded seedlings should be thinned ruthlessly if their foliage is touching. When vegetables grow too close together, leafy plants become stunted, root crops become distorted, and vine crops give poor growth because of self-shading, and the yields of large crops are reduced. Furthermore, it is easier for pests and diseases to damage overcrowded crops.

Thinnings of leaf crops can, of course, be eaten. Or they can make good compost.

SETTING OUT TRANSPLANTS

If you germinate seeds indoors in a flat, you'll have to face the fact that transplanting the seedlings to a garden bed can present problems.

The chief difficulty with setting out seedlings is transplant shock—seedlings will not grow and may drop some leaves until new feeder roots get established. Recovery may take several days. The trauma may be severe and prolonged if the plants are separated roughly from a thickly planted seedling pan and are not hardened-off.

To reduce transplanting shock, transplant seedlings from flats to small, soil-filled peat pots indoors and harden-off plants outdoors before transplanting them to the garden. (Or sprout seeds in peat pots from the beginning.)

When to transplant

Cold-resistant plants, such as cabbage, broccoli, and onions, may be transplanted to the garden after hardening-off even if occasional light spring frosts are expected. Transplanting of celery should be delayed until danger of frost is past. Heavy frost can trigger the mechanism that causes celery to go to seed instead of growing vegetatively.

Unless a protective covering is used, the transplanting of warmth-loving plants, such as pepper, eggplant, melon, cucumber, squash, and tomato, should be delayed until after all danger of frost is past and the soil has warmed up.

It is always best to transplant in the cool of late afternoon or early evening. If the job must be done in the warm sunlight, give the plants the temporary shade of a shingle or paper.

Reduce transplant shock by setting seedlings outdoors on warm days. Chicken wire cover foils birds.

Transplanting procedures

When setting out purchased or home-grown seedlings or very small seedlings thinned from garden rows, follow these steps:

1) Dig holes for receiving the plants and fill them with water; let it soak in.

2) Water plants thoroughly. If you are using peat pots, soak them until they are moist and soft before you set them out in the garden.

3) If the plants are not in individual pots, carefully separate the root ball of each plant from the larger soil mass, preserving as much soil around the roots as possible. If a plant in an individual pot is rootbound, rough up the roots with your fingers before planting. Trim off any roots that are very long.

4) If the plants are quite large, trim off about half the leaves to reduce the loss of water. Don't trim the central growing tip.

5) Until they are planted, cover roots with a damp cloth to prevent them from drying. Even brief drying can damage delicate feeder roots.

6) Set in the plants to the original depth or *slightly* deeper than they grew in the soil. Planting too deep can slow or stop plant growth. Tomatoes are exceptions—you can bury from half to three-quarters of their stems (see photo on page 40).

7) Cover the roots with loose soil drawn up around them and gently firmed down. Tug at the tip of a leaf.

Protecting transplants

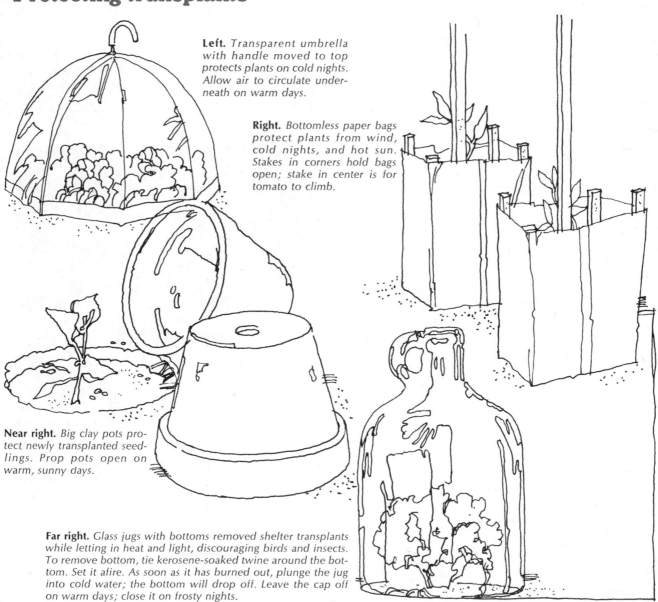

Left. *Transparent umbrella with handle moved to top protects plants on cold nights. Allow air to circulate underneath on warm days.*

Right. *Bottomless paper bags protect plants from wind, cold nights, and hot sun. Stakes in corners hold bags open; stake in center is for tomato to climb.*

Near right. *Big clay pots protect newly transplanted seedlings. Prop pots open on warm, sunny days.*

Far right. *Glass jugs with bottoms removed shelter transplants while letting in heat and light, discouraging birds and insects. To remove bottom, tie kerosene-soaked twine around the bottom. Set it afire. As soon as it has burned out, plunge the jug into cold water; the bottom will drop off. Leave the cap off on warm days; close it on frosty nights.*

If the plant stirs, firm the soil again. The leaf tip should come off in your fingers before the plant will move. Don't mound the soil up, though, or it will shed water.

8) Water again to settle the soil around the roots. If you haven't added a high-phosphate fertilizer during soil preparation, the use of a high-phosphate starter solution will aid in root formation.

When moving established plants from one location in the garden to another, follow this procedure:

1) Dig the transplanting holes slightly oversize; fill them with water and let it soak in.

2) Move the plants, taking a shovelful of soil with each.

3) Test the depth of the hole while the plant is still in the shovel; if it's too deep, fill it in with loose soil.

4) Set in the plant and pull loose soil up around it.

5) Don't firm the root ball itself or you may break the roots. Gently firm the soil around the roots.

6) Settle the soil by watering.

Continuing care of transplants

If it doesn't rain, water transplants daily for the first week. Water plants with a weak solution of high-phosphate fertilizer to get them growing fast.

Protect young seedlings by using collars that prevent cutworms from chewing the plants off at the surface of the soil. For small plants make collars of juice cans, milk cartons, stiff cardboard, or aluminum foil. Slip the tubes over the plants and twist them firmly into the soil.

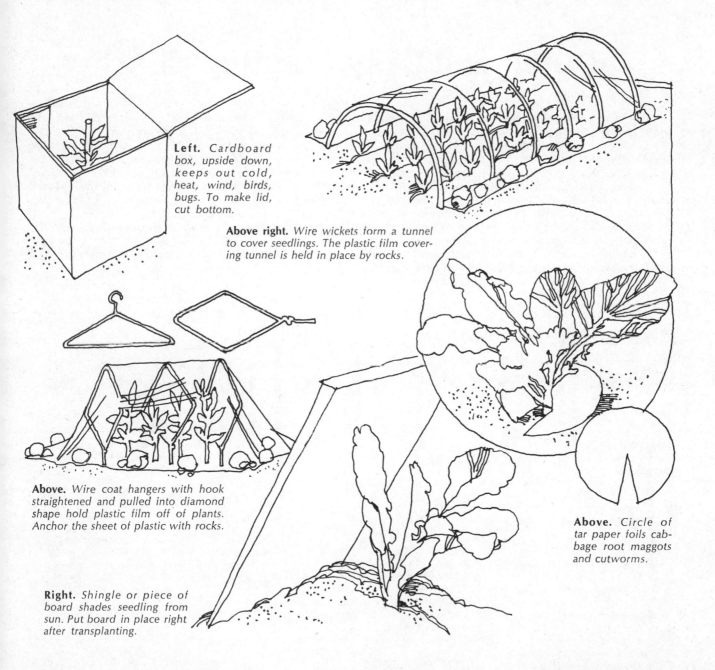

Left. *Cardboard box, upside down, keeps out cold, heat, wind, birds, bugs. To make lid, cut bottom.*

Above right. *Wire wickets form a tunnel to cover seedlings. The plastic film covering tunnel is held in place by rocks.*

Above. *Wire coat hangers with hook straightened and pulled into diamond shape hold plastic film off of plants. Anchor the sheet of plastic with rocks.*

Right. *Shingle or piece of board shades seedling from sun. Put board in place right after transplanting.*

Above. *Circle of tar paper foils cabbage root maggots and cutworms.*

Tomatoes *are the only exception to the planting depth rule. Their stem goes deeply into hole (see page 38).*

Soak peat pot *well before setting it into the planting hole. Continue to water within the pot rim.*

Quick and Easy Planting Chart

In this chart you'll find the general information needed for planning your garden. When the time comes to plant, look for more detailed information under each vegetable listed in the Gardener's Guide, pp. 56-95.

The first three columns show the recommended method for planting—indoors in containers or outdoors in the ground—as well as the season to plant. If information appears in the first column, this means that planting seeds indoors or in a hotbed (see page 31) is recommended for starting that vegetable. The second column tells you when to transplant your own seedlings or plants bought at the nursery. (Rely on indoor plant-ing where the growing season is very short and you need a head start or when seeds are very small and the outdoor germination rate is low. Buying plants is practical when you are only growing a few.)

Columns three through seven give information on planting seeds outdoors. In column eight, the distance between transplants/seedlings applies to both setting out plants and thinning seedlings.

The time needed for seeds to sprout will vary with the soil temperature. Use harvest date information for general planning only—it will vary with the variety planted, your locality, and time of sowing.

Vegetable	Weeks before last frost to plant seeds indoors	Set out transplants	Plant seeds outdoors	Days from planting to sprouting	Soil temperature for starting seeds	Depth to plant seeds	Distance apart to plant seeds	Distance between transplants/seedlings	From seed to harvest (*From setting out transplant)	Comments
Artichokes	N	Early spring-midsummer	N	N	N	N	N	4'	1 yr.*	Perennial. Grow from plants or roots.
Asparagus	N	Fall, winter, early spring	N	N	N	N	N	1-2'	2 yrs.*	Perennial. 3 yrs. from seed. Grow from plant or roots.
Beans **Bush snap**	N	N	Midspring-early summer	7-14	65-75°	1"	3"	4-6"	50-60 days	All beans need warm weather.
Pole snap	N	N	Midspring-early summer	7-14	65-75°	1"	3"	1'	60-70 days	Produce over a longer period.

N = not recommended or applicable.

Vegetable	Weeks before last frost to plant seeds indoors	Set out transplants	Plant seeds outdoors	Days from planting to sprouting	Soil temperature for starting seeds	Depth to plant seeds	Distance apart to plant seeds	Distance between transplants/seedlings	From seed to harvest (*From setting out transplant)	Comments
Beans										
Bush lima	N	N	Early-midsummer	14-21	70-80°	1″	4″	1′	65-75 days	Need long, warm summers.
Pole lima	N	N	Early-midsummer	14-21	70-80°	1″	6″	1′	80-95 days	Where warm season is short, start indoors in peat pots.
Beets	N	N	After frost-fall	14-21	65-75°	½″	1″	3″	46-65 days	No tolerance for hot weather.
Broccoli	5-7	After frost, late summer-fall	Early spring, midsummer	7-14	60-75°	½″	1″	2½-3′	50-90 days*	Cool weather only.
Brussels sprouts	4-6	After frost, late summer-fall	Late summer-fall	7-14	60-75°	½″	3″	3′	80-90 days*	Cool weather only.
Cabbage	5-7	After frost, late summer	Midsummer	7-14	60-75°	½″	3″	1-2′	50-80 days	Cool weather only.
Chinese cabbage	N	N	Midsummer	7-14	60-75°	½″	3″	1′	65-80 days	Cool weather only. Do not transplant.
Carrots	N	N	Early spring-fall	14-21	65-75°	½″	½″	2″	65-75 days	Keep seedbed moist. Prefer cool weather.
Cauliflower	5-7	After frost, late summer-fall	N	7-14	60-75°	½″	3″	18-20″	60-100 days*	Cool weather only.
Celery	10-12	After frost, late summer	N	14-21	65-75°	⅛″	1″	6″	100-135 days*	Cool weather only.
Chard, Swiss	N	N	Early spring-late summer	14-21	65-75°	½″	1″	12″	45-60 days	Tolerates summer heat.
Collards	N	N	Mid-late spring, late summer-fall	7-14	60-75°	½″	1″	18-24″	75-85 days	Spring planting only in North.
Corn										
Early	N	N	Early-late summer	7-14	55-70°	1″	2″	6″	60-65 days	Plant where warm season is short.
Mid-season	N	N	Early-midsummer	7-14	60-80°	1″	3″	8″	65-80 days	Medium-size ears.
Late	N	N	Early summer	7-14	60-80°	1″	4″	12-18″	80-90 days	Usually larger plants and ears.
Cress	N	N	Early-mid-spring	7-14	60-75°	½″	1″	3″	45 days	Watercress grows 50 days to harvest.
Cucumbers	N	N	Early-midsummer	7-14	70-80°	1″	2-3″	12″	55-65 days	Warm weather only.

N = not recommended or applicable.

Planting chart 41

Vegetable	Weeks before last frost to plant seeds indoors	Set out transplants	Plant seeds outdoors	Days from planting to sprouting	Soil temperature for starting seeds	Depth to plant seeds	Distance apart to plant seeds	Distance between transplants/seedlings	From seed to harvest (*From setting out transplant)	Comments
Eggplant	8-9	Midspring-early summer	N	14-21	75-80°	¼"	½"	3'	65-80 days*	Indoors, plant 8-10 weeks before last frost.
Endive	N	N	Early spring, late summer	14-21	65-75°	¼"	1"	12-18'	65-90 days	Prefers cool weather.
Garlic	N	N	Early spring, winter	7-14	60-75°	1"	2"	3'	80-90 days	Grow from sets (cloves).
Horseradish	N	Fall, late winter, early spring	N	14-28	N	N	N	1'	9 months*	Plant roots 2" below soil surface.
Jerusalem artichoke	N	Fall, early spring	N	14-28	N	N	N	10-18"	9-11 months*	Plant tubers 2-4" deep.
Kale	N	N	Early spring, late summer	7-14	60-75°	½"	1"	6-12"	60-70 days	Tolerates frosts.
Kohlrabi	N	N	Early-late spring, late summer-fall	7-14	60-75°	2"	6"	12"	55-65 days	Use greens from thinnings.
Leeks	10-12	Early summer, late summer	Mid-late spring	14-21	60-75°	¼"	½"	3-4"	80-90 days*	Dislike temperature extremes.
Lettuce Leaf	N	N	Early-late spring, late summer-fall	14-21	55-65°	½"	1"	6"	40-45 days	Takes more heat than other lettuce types.
Romaine	N	N	Late summer-fall	14-21	55-65°	½"	½"	8"	70-85 days	Tolerates some heat.
Head	3-5	After frost	Late summer-fall	14-21	55-65°	½"	½"	1'	80-95 days	Needs long, cool season.
Melons (Except watermelons)	3-4	Mid-late spring	Early-midsummer	14-21	75-80°	1"	4"	3-8'	80-95 days	Indoors, plant in peat pots. Need long, warm season.
Mustard greens	N	N	Early spring, late summer-fall	7-14	60-75°	½"	2"	2'	35-60 days	Prefer cool weather.
Okra	N	Early summer	Early mid-summer	14-21	70-80°	1"	12"	3'	50-60 days	Soak seeds before planting.
Onions Bunching (Green onions)	N	N	Early spring-fall	14-21	60-75°	¼"	½"	1"	60-75 days	Harvest 25-50 days from plants.
Bulbing (Dry onions)	6-8	After frost	After frost	14-21	60-75°	¼"	½"	4"	100-120 days	Harvest 50-70 days from sets.
Parsley	8-10	After frost-late spring, late summer	Early-late spring	21-28	65-75°	¼"	½"	18"	70-90 days	Biennial. Soak seeds before planting.

N = not recommended or applicable.

Vegetable	Weeks before last frost to plant seeds indoors	Set out transplants	Plant seeds outdoors	Days from planting to sprouting	Soil temperature for starting seeds	Depth to plant seeds	Distance apart to plant seeds	Distance between transplants/seedlings	From seed to harvest (*From setting out transplant)	Comments
Parsnips	N	N	Mid-late spring, fall	21-28	60-75°	¼ "	½ "	6"	100-120 days	Takes frost.
Peanuts	N	N	Early-midsummer	7-14	70-80°	1½ "	3"	6"	110-120 days	Use peat pots indoors.
Peas	N	N	After frost, fall	7-14	50-60°	1"	2"	3"	60-70 days	Cool weather only.
Peppers	8-10	Midspring-early summer	N	14-21	70-80°	⅛ "	1"	18"	60-80 days	Start 8-10 weeks before transplanting time.
Potatoes	N	N	Early spring, late summer	7-14	N	N	N	18"	90-105 days	Plant sets.
Pumpkins	N	N	Early-midsummer	7-14	65-75°	1"	3"	3'	100-120 days	Warm weather only.
Radishes	N	N	Early spring-fall	7-14	45-70°	½ "	1"	1"	20-50 days	Plant winter varieties in the fall.
Rhubarb	N	After frost	N	N	N	N	N	4-6'	2 yrs. 1 yr. from roots.	Plant roots in early spring. Perennial.
Rutabaga	N	N	Mid-late spring, late summer	7-14	50-65°	½ "	1"	1'	90 days	Best as a fall crop.
Salsify	N	N	Mid-late spring	14-21	65-75°	½ "	2"	6"	120-150 days	Will store in ground in winter.
Shallots	N	Early spring, fall	Early spring, fall	7-14	N	N	N	3"	150 days	Grow from sets.
Spinach	N	N	After frost, late summer	7-14	40-55°	½ "	1"	8"	40-50 days	Prefers cool weather.
Squash Summer	N	N	Early-midsummer	7-14	65-80°	1-2"	2"	4'	50-60 days	Warm weather only.
Winter	N	N	Early-midsummer	7-14	65-80°	1-2"	3"	6-8'	80-120 days	Pick before frost.
Tomatoes	6-8	Midspring-early summer	N	14-21	75-80°	¼ "	2"	2-4'	55-90* days	Match variety to climate. Try hybrids.
Turnips	N	N	Early-late spring, late summer	7-14	50-65°	¼ "	1"	6"	35-60 days	Prefer cool weather.
Watermelon	2-3	After frost	Early-midsummer	7-14	70-75°	1"	2"	6-8'	70-90 days	Indoors, plant in peat pots.

N = not recommended or applicable.

Care and Feeding of Your Crops

To produce quality vegetables, your plants need ample water and nutrients and freedom from weeds and pests. A plant started at the right time of year for that crop, planted in rich soil, and given the right amount of water and fertilizer will not only produce the best vegetables but also will be the most resistant to any problems that come along.

As you get to know the plants you are growing, you'll learn to spot their need for watering, feeding, or shading from a hot sun. Pull weeds as they pop up; water before your plants look as if they need it; pick or hose off any damaging bugs when you see them. You'll find that this regular attention goes a long way toward eliminating major chores by heading off trouble before it starts.

Sheet shades lettuce *on hot day, keeps it from going to seed.*

WATERING

Good-tasting vegetables require a steady supply of moisture for uninterrupted growth from seedling to harvest. Too much water will encourage foliage rather than fruit development; too much can also suffocate the roots so they're unable to grow. On the other hand, allowing the roots to dry out will stop growth completely and damage or kill the plant quickly on a hot day. Your watering goal is to keep the moisture level as even as possible, penetrating the soil below root depth and repeating before the soil dries out enough to cause wilting.

How much water?

To determine how much and how often to water plants in your garden, consider such factors as climate, type of soil, and rooting depths of plants. Weekly watering might be enough in cool, damp climates, but your garden will probably need watering daily in hot, dry regions.

Regardless of the weather, how often you water depends on the water-holding capacity of your soil. Soils composed of coarse particles hold less water than soils made up of fine particles. For example, a sandy soil must be watered more frequently than a clay soil.

Test how deeply water penetrates the soil with a trowel for shallow-rooted vegetables and with a metal rod or soil sampling tube for deeper ones.

In an average loam, an inch of water applied at the surface will wet the soil to a depth of 4 to 5 inches (more in sandy soil, less in clay soil). Since even many small vegetables may root to a 12-inch depth, you should apply at least 3 inches of water. Large vegetables feed mainly in the top 12 inches of soil but send out roots to depths of 3 feet or more for anchoring and some water absorption. Apply 6 to 9 inches of water to penetrate to these depths.

If you pond water in deep furrows between beds, you can roughly measure how much water you apply by gauging the depth of the furrow. When you water with a sprinkler, measure applications in a glass set halfway between the sprinkler and its maximum reach.

Watering methods

A combination of overhead sprinkling and directly soaking the soil is the way most gardeners water their plants. A new method that uses porous plastic pipes is expensive to install but saves water in the long run.

Overhead watering. Using a good sprinkler that distributes water evenly over the entire surface of the ground is a time-saving way to water a big garden, and many

Furrow watering *gives large, thirsty vegetables the deep soaking they need. Dig them at planting time.*

Sprinkling *suits French intensive mounded bed. Posts keep hose from knocking over crops in other beds.*

crops thrive under overhead sprinkling.

But overhead watering has some disadvantages, too. Moisture on leaves can encourage rust or mildew in some crops. On very hot days, water on the foliage can cause scalding. Water is also wasted during overhead sprinkling through instant evaporation and splashing. If you do sprinkle, wait until the wind is calm and water in the morning so plants will dry off by evening.

Soaking the soil. For most gardens, slow soaking of water into the soil is the safest method. It works well for level beds or terraced slopes and in small gardens where you want to avoid sprinkling certain vegetables. An additional advantage of watering in furrows is that you avoid compacting the whole surface of the garden. That saves a lot of cultivating.

Except in sandy soils, furrow watering is an efficient method for beds where plants are positioned no more than 3 to 4 inches in from the shoulder of the furrow, since the lateral wetting of the soil doesn't go much beyond this. Dig the furrows before planting, making them up to a foot wide and 6 inches deep. Lay them out so they're as level as possible.

Send water into the furrows as slowly as possible so that water can penetrate evenly and soil won't wash away. Penetration will be increased if you divide long furrows into 6-foot segments on sandy soil or 12-foot segments on heavier, less permeable soils. Use a dam made of a board, a piece of metal, or a wide shovel placed upright in the furrow to hold the water until a section of the furrow has been soaked. As the plants grow, move some soil gradually from the sides and bot-

Simplify your watering chores

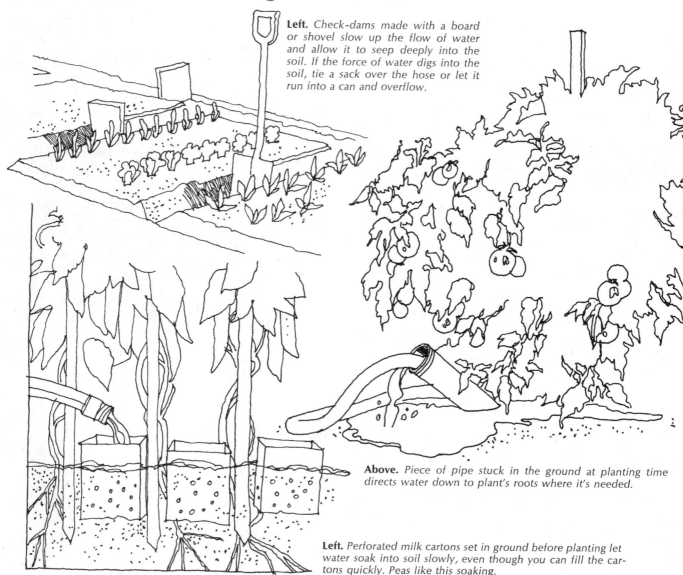

Left. Check-dams made with a board or shovel slow up the flow of water and allow it to seep deeply into the soil. If the force of water digs into the soil, tie a sack over the hose or let it run into a can and overflow.

Above. Piece of pipe stuck in the ground at planting time directs water down to plant's roots where it's needed.

Left. Perforated milk cartons set in ground before planting let water soak into soil slowly, even though you can fill the cartons quickly. Peas like this soaking.

tom of the furrow to the base of the plants to replace any soil that water has eroded away and to help hold plants up.

Watering basins are useful for large, spreading vines, such as cucumbers and melons. (Plant several seeds in each center mound and eventually thin to three plants.) By confining the water inside the basin and guiding the vines outside it, you will help keep the fruit from rotting on soggy ground.

Drip irrigation. Systems for applying small, steady amounts of water to a crop are being used by commercial growers to conserve water and save labor but can be adapted to home gardens, especially for large vegetables. In this system, fittings on above-ground plastic pipes drip continuously onto the soil. Some systems require pressure regulators and filters and tend to clog

with algae unless pipes are impregnated with a retardant or are flushed regularly. Look for the type that has grooved plastic attachments without holes that can be clogged. The size of the attachment can be changed, depending on the size of the crop. These systems are distributed through commercial orchard suppliers.

MULCHING

Covering the soil with a mulch can help maintain an even moisture level in the soil, as well as conserve water by reducing evaporation. Once the soil has warmed up, mulching will reduce the fluctuation in soil temperature that can harm the plants. Spreading a mulch over the soil will greatly reduce the need for weeding. Mulches reduce the need for cultivating by stopping a

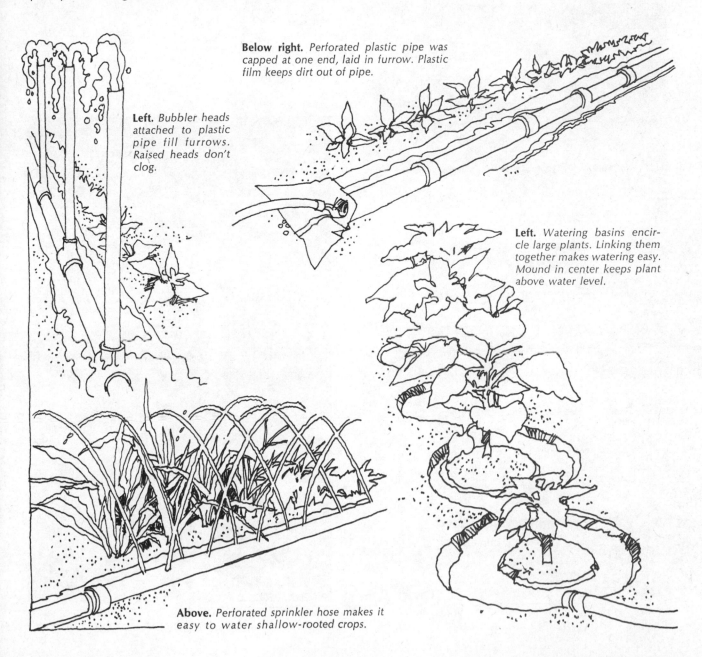

Below right. *Perforated plastic pipe was capped at one end, laid in furrow. Plastic film keeps dirt out of pipe.*

Left. *Bubbler heads attached to plastic pipe fill furrows. Raised heads don't clog.*

Left. *Watering basins encircle large plants. Linking them together makes watering easy. Mound in center keeps plant above water level.*

Above. *Perforated sprinkler hose makes it easy to water shallow-rooted crops.*

soil crust from forming. A mulch will also keep mud from splattering on leafy vegetables.

Several precautions:
• Don't apply a mulch to young seedlings—it may keep them damp enough to rot.
• Keep mulches away from plants that might suffer crown rot, such as root crops.
• Mulches provide hiding spots for some trouble-makers; watch out for slugs and sowbugs.
• Don't use a mulch while the ground is still cold, or the mulch will prevent the soil from warming up. (However, a covering of hay in the winter can retard the freezing of winter vegetables and allow you to store root vegetables in the ground.)

Organic mulches. Mulches made of organic materials add nutrients and humus to the soil as they slowly decompose. This means that you must replenish them periodically. This continual process keeps the topsoil in prime condition for root growth, making it easier to prepare the bed each time you plant.

As a mulch, use the materials you can obtain easily and inexpensively in your area. Here are some favorites:
• Well-rotted manure. Will burn plants if too fresh. May contain weed seeds, excess salts.
• Leaves. Shredded leaves don't mat down. Commercial leaf mold is expensive, but you can make your own by composting dried leaves and fresh grass clippings. Shredding the leaves speeds decomposition.

(Continued on page 50)

If you see *damage from bugs, pull mulch away from plants—it makes a good hiding place for them.*

Water *from plastic pipes goes into holes punched in black plastic mulch next to each plant.*

Newspapers *make an inexpensive mulch. Cover them with soil to keep them from blowing away.*

Keeping out the creatures

If your garden has become a salad bar for rabbits, gophers, or deer, the most effective solution is to fence them out. Raised beds lined with ½-inch hardware cloth or aviary wire on the bottom will keep such burrowers as gophers or moles away from succulent roots.

A rabbit-proof fence should be at least 2 feet tall and go at least 6 inches underground. Rabbits can burrow under that, but you should be able to notice the holes before the animals get all the way under. Mesh on the chicken wire should be no wider than 1½ inches.

A deer-proof fence should be at least 8 feet high. If your building code doesn't allow this, an outrigger structure will discourage deer—they don't like to jump very far.

If you live in an area where you have many of these persistent visitors, a cage might be the answer to keeping all of them away, including birds. As a bonus, the cage can be covered with a sheet or other material to protect winter crops from frosty nights and cool-season crops from hot weather.

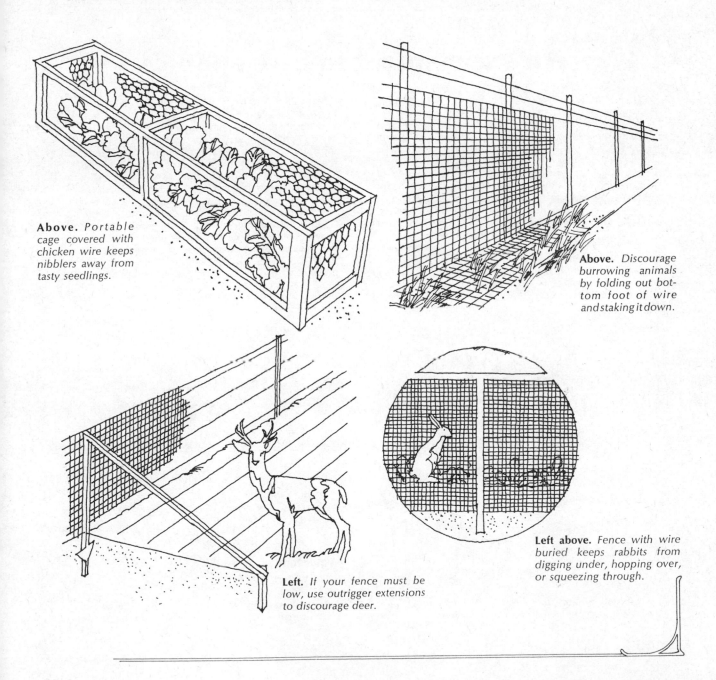

Above. *Portable cage covered with chicken wire keeps nibblers away from tasty seedlings.*

Above. *Discourage burrowing animals by folding out bottom foot of wire and staking it down.*

Left. *If your fence must be low, use outrigger extensions to discourage deer.*

Left above. *Fence with wire buried keeps rabbits from digging under, hopping over, or squeezing through.*

- Straw or hay. Add a high nitrogen fertilizer to the soil before mulching.
- Wood shavings, chips, bark, or sawdust. Add a nitrogen fertilizer to the soil before mulching if it hasn't already been added to the packaged product.
- Newspapers. Use six sheets to each layer and overlap generously to stop weeds. Cover the edges with soil to keep the papers from blowing away. Add a nitrogen fertilizer to the soil before mulching. Newspapers take at least several months to decay and often much longer; any left at the end of the season can be plowed into the soil.

- Lawn clippings. Spread a thin layer to dry; if applied too quickly, they will quickly mat down and become slimy, develop odors, and attract flies.

Plastic mulch. Polyethylene film will do everything that other mulches do except add organic matter to the soil. Use black plastic; sunlight will penetrate clear plastic and weed growth will continue. Black plastic prevents weed growth and warms the soil as long as the sun is shining on it.

You can use plastic mulch to cover the spaces between planting rows, or you can punch holes directly

An experiment in hydroponics

Hydroponics means "working water," and, although you can choose among many methods, all of them work on the same principle: the plant receives all of its nutrients from the watering solution instead of from the soil.

To try this yourself, start several seeds with any of the methods described on pages 29-31. When secondary leaves appear on the seedlings, transplant each into a pot filled with lightweight gravel to one inch of the top. The container should have a cork or stopper for the drainage hole. Mix a commercial hydroponic plant food according to directions on the package, making enough solution to fill the container to the top of the gravel.

Twice a day, water the plant with the solution, leaving the plug in the drainage hole until the container is full. Then pull the plug, catching the excess in a bucket or pan to use for the next feeding. Repeat this schedule for a week; then mix up a new batch and continue to feed twice a day. The plant food supplies all the nutrients that the plant needs to grow and produce fruit.

Other methods use planting mediums that are more conventional. For an indoor container, try half peat moss and half vermiculite as a planting mix. Feed each plant 8 ounces of nutrient solution every other day.

Outdoors, fill a raised bed or planter box with 1 part sand and 3 parts sawdust. Feed each plant 8 ounces of nutrient solution once a week and water twice a week with plain water (three times a week in hot weather).

Once you succeed with a plant grown hydroponically, you might want to try one of the devices available that make the feeding automatic. These range from single containers to greenhouse units with pump, timers, and hoses—the ultimate in hydroponics. With these, you can plant a cherry tomato seedling and not touch it again until the tomatoes are ready.

Nutrient solution *drains out of planter through hose, back into bucket where it's ready for re-use.*

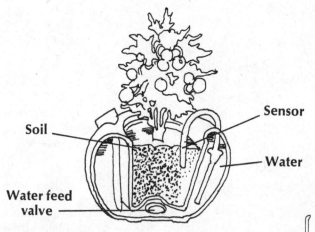

Automatic watering *and feeding device keeps moisture and nutrients at correct level for healthy growth.*

in it to sow seeds or set out transplants. Weight down the plastic with rocks or cover the edges with a thin layer of soil.

WEEDING

No one in full command of his senses would probably ever feel that weeding is fun. But it is one of the most important and necessary garden chores. Weeds rob surrounding vegetables of food and water and compete with young plants for sunlight. And there are aesthetic reasons for weeding too; many people maintain very clean gardens because they like everything neat and orderly.

Hand-pulling, hoeing, and cultivating are all good methods for getting rid of weeds. Hand-pulling and hoeing are best in small gardens; cultivating is more practical in large ones. Avoid cultivating too deeply so you don't disturb feeder roots of vegetables. Dig out deep-rooted weeds with a weeding tool.

Here are some labor-saving weeding points:
• Pull weed seedlings as soon as they appear.
• Hoe weeds in dry soil to kill roots faster.
• Weeds pulled by hand come out more easily when the soil is moist.
• Never let weeds mature through their growing cycle so they go to seed.
• Gather and compost weeds to keep them from taking root in the garden again after being pulled up.
• Avoid using weed-control chemicals near vegetables; they can drift by wind or water and harm your plants.

FERTILIZING

All vegetables can benefit from the nutrients a fertilizer will supply. The three major nutrients a plant needs are nitrogen, phosphorus, and potassium. Nitrogen stimulates rapid growth of stems and leaves. Phosphorus encourages root formation, flowering, and fruiting. Potassium (potash) is essential to all plant life processes.

To get vegetables off to a fast start, work a fertilizer high in phosphorus into the soil when you prepare it. When you set out transplants, water them with a high-phosphate solution. After seedlings are well established, feed them with a nitrogen-rich fertilizer to speed their growth.

Which fertilizer?

Ultimately all fertilizers, whether they are organic or manufactured substances, are broken down into simple inorganic chemicals before plants can use them. Generally, organic fertilizers improve the soil structure and release their foods slowly. Manufactured fertilizers do not improve soil structure, but they are ready for a plant to use almost as soon as they are added to the soil.

Sack of manure *hangs in tub; add water and soak to make liquid manure. Dilute to use as fertilizer.*

Organic fertilizers

What most people mean when they say "organic fertilizer" is a plant food derived from some animal, vegetable, or mineral source.

Here are some of the most common organic sources of the three major nutrients:
• Nitrogen: blood meal, hoof and horn meal, cottonseed meal, fish meal, fish emulsion, activated sewage sludge, animal manures, bone meal
• Phosphorus: bone meal, phosphate rock
• Potassium: granite dust, pulverized granite, potash rock, wood ashes

Organic fertilizers are most effective when worked into the soil and release more nutrients when the soil is warm. A good time to correct any nutrient deficiencies in the soil is when you are preparing the planting bed. Generous amounts of aged manure and compost will improve both soil structure and soil fertility. Working phosphate rock into the root zone will make this nutrient available to young roots.

(Continued on next page)

Vegetables in a haystack

If your soil is hopeless and you can find a supply of hay, you can grow vegetables while you're waiting for the hay to decompose. Select the site for your hay garden carefully—it can attract flies.

Push the bales of hay together, soak them with water and cover the tops with a 3 to 4-inch layer of poultry manure. Make holes in the manure, fill these with a potting soil mix, and set in the plants. (Robust vegetables, such as tomatoes, eggplants, squash, and cucumbers, work best with this method.) The soil mix on top of the manure will buffer the roots from the harsh manure until watering reduces the ammonia and salts to tolerable levels for the plants.

Soak the bales every few days—the hay must be kept moist enough to accept the vegetables' roots. The vegetables will cascade over the bales with very little competition from weeds. By the end of the growing season, the partially decomposed hay can be composted or used as a starter for the top of next year's bales.

When plants are established, feed them with a high nitrogen fertilizer, such as fish emulsion. This also benefits transplants. Mix and apply according to the directions on the label.

Manufactured fertilizers

Artificially made fertilizers offer two distinct advantages. Most are ready faster than organic fertilizers for plants to use. And they are usually less expensive, since they are more concentrated and since you apply a smaller amount. Check labels for a fertilizer recommended for vegetables.

Granular, water-soluble, high-nitrogen fertilizers should be applied monthly for best results—every two weeks on sandy soils. If you sprinkler-irrigate, dig shallow furrows parallel to the rows, 3 to 6 inches from the plants. Apply the fertilizer in a band, working it into the soil. Don't let any fertilizer touch the foliage.

WHAT'S BEEN EATING MY LETTUCE?

Pests and diseases particularly bothersome to each vegetable are listed in the Gardener's Guide, pages 56-95. Use the methods described there if pests begin to do actual damage. Following are general precautions you can take to discourage damage to your crops:

• Plant disease-resistant varieties if available. Resistant hybrids have been developed for the most troublesome vegetable diseases. Many excellent tomato hybrids, for example, are resistant to verticillium and fusarium wilt.

• Encourage healthy plant growth by providing optimum growing conditions. Rich, well-drained soil will support the kind of healthy plant that is less susceptible to attacks of insects or diseases.

• Keep your garden tidy. Clean up debris that can become breeding and hiding places for harmful creatures. Inspect mulch for signs of insects and pull the mulch away from the plant if you see any signs of trouble.

• Don't concentrate crops in just one place. Large expanses of one type of plant encourage pests that thrive on that plant. Mixed plantings may make it harder for insects to locate the crops they feed on by confusing their sense of smell. Mixed plantings also can sustain a greater array of friendly insects (parasites and predators of the bad guys).

• Look carefully; then leap. While you're watering, weeding, and harvesting your crops, keep a watchful eye out for the first signs of damage. If you see a big troublemaker in action, pick it off and destroy it. Wash small insects off with a strong jet of water from the hose. If the damage is being done by such night creatures as snails, slugs, and cutworms, you will have to look for them at night with a flashlight or trap them under boards or in sheets of rolled-up newspapers and dispose of them.

(Continued on page 54)

Strong jet *from the hose washes off bean pests. Try this on insects too small to pick off by hand.*

Now, about those pests

Use this page to identify the most common vegetable pests. (And consult your county farm advisor about local pest problems.) Once you know what's doing the damage, check the listing for a particular vegetable in the Gardener's Guide (pages 56-95) to learn any special considerations for dealing with pests that plant may attract. If you have tried removing the pest by hand or by hose and it continues to do serious damage to the crop, spray with a product that specifies on its label that it can be used for vegetables. Allow the recommended time between spraying and harvest.

If you find holes in your leaves . . .

SNAILS AND SLUGS

Find them eating at night and on overcast days and pick them off. Sprinkle ashes around plants. Set out boards; check during the day. Use snail bait.

BEAN BEETLE

Pick them off of foliage. Some of them feed at night—look for them by flashlight. Use rotenone, malathion, sevin, ryania, or diazinon.

CUCUMBER BEETLE

Find these on squash and melons as well as cucumbers and pick them off. Use rotenone, malathion, sevin, or diazinon.

CABBAGE WORM

Hand pick them from cabbage, broccoli, Brussels sprouts, cauliflower. Use Bacillus thuringiensis, rotenone, or malathion before heads form.

If tiny bugs suck plant juices . . .

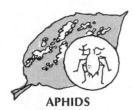

APHIDS

These can be green, black, yellow, or pink. Hose off with water or soap solution. Use rotenone, malathion, ryania, pyrethrum or sevin.

LEAFHOPPERS

Fast-moving green or brownish bugs feed on underside of leaf, causing white stippling on top. Common on beans. Use malathion or sevin.

SPIDER MITES

Finely stippled leaves with silvery webs on underside; you need a hand lens to see the mites. Wash them off. Use malathion or diazinon.

WHITEFLIES

Look for them on the underside of leaves, especially on beans and tomatoes. Hose off with water or soap solution. Use malathion or rotenone.

If borers eat into leaves and fruit . . .

LEAF MINERS

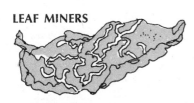

Insects lay eggs on leaf surface. Larvae enter leaves; feeding results in a serpentine trail. Pick off infested leaves. Use rotenone.

CORN EARWORM

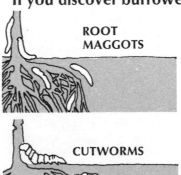

These crawl into the ear of corn. Cut silks 3 days after ears reach full size. Put mineral oil on silks (see page 69). Use ryania.

If you discover burrowers in the soil . . .

ROOT MAGGOTS

Commonly found on the cabbage family and root crops. Use a tarpaper collar (see page 39). Use diazinon around seedlings.

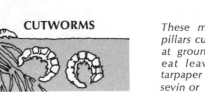

CUTWORMS

These moth caterpillars cut off stems at ground level or eat leaves. Use a tarpaper collar. Use sevin or diazinon.

Pests 53

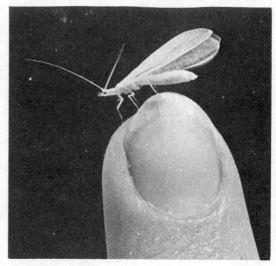

Lacewing larva *grabs aphid and sucks juice until only the body hull remains. Larvae also eat other small bugs.*

Adult lacewing *eats no bugs but starts laying eggs soon after emerging from the cocoon.*

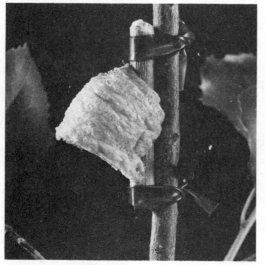

Attach mantis egg case *to sturdy stem. Each case will produce about 50 mantises.*

Praying mantis *eats aphids, whiteflies, and spider mites. Mantises lay their eggs then die after one season.*

• Encourage natural controls. Many birds, toads, and lizards eat insects. You can buy some beneficial insects from mail-order sources (ladybugs, praying mantises, lacewings, and trichogramma wasps). Don't depend on these insects to wipe out your entire pest population— it's possible that they'll fly over the fence at the first opportunity. If you have a wide variety of pests for them to feed on, though, these good insects may colonize and cut down considerably on crop damage. Ladybugs, lacewings, and praying mantises concentrate on aphids and other soft-bodied insects. Trichogramma wasps destroy moth eggs before they hatch into cabbage loopers and other leaf-eating caterpillars.

• Aromatic plants, such as garlic, onions, hot peppers, and marigolds, may ward off some pests with their strong odors. Plant them around the vegetables that seem most susceptible to damage.

• Spray or dust only as a last resort. You should use sprays only if a specific pest gets out of hand on a particular crop. Slight damage to crops is not the signal to start a chemical war. Learn to accept a few holes in the lettuce or a few plants lost to the troublemakers.

Homemade sprays. Some gardeners have found that a soap mixture sprayed on the plant will destroy mealybugs and aphids. Mix 9 level tablespoons of old-fashioned soap flakes, not detergent, in 3 gallons of water.

You can try discouraging other insects by blending equal parts of strong smelling plants such as hot peppers, onions, garlic, or marigolds with an equal amount of water. Strain out the liquid and use 1 teaspoon of the liquid extract to a pint of water.

Botanical sprays. Rotenone, pyrethrum, and ryania are toxic to insects but relatively safe to man. Because they have little residual effect, you must apply them directly to the insect. They control some of the common sucking and chewing insects, such as beetles, whiteflies, and aphids.

Manufactured chemicals. Only three manufactured insecticides on the market should be used by home gardeners on vegetables: sevin, diazanon, and malathion. These should be applied strictly according to label directions. They are most effective against sucking insects such as aphids, thrips, leaf hoppers, and whiteflies. Many sprays for vegetables contain a mixture of these chemicals—check the label to be sure that the formulation you use is certified for edible crops. *Never* use any spray that isn't specifically recommended on the label for vegetables. Follow the directions *exactly* as to how long before harvest you must spray.

Biological controls. Certain bacterial cultures can kill specific insects without harm to warm-blooded creatures. Several manufacturers offer products containing *Bacillus thuringiensis*, which can control several insects in their caterpillar stage. "Milky spore disease" spores are available for control of Japanese beetles.

HARVESTING AND STORING YOUR VEGETABLES

Follow the recommendations under each vegetable in the *Gardener's Guide* (pages 56-95) for harvesting each at its peak of tenderness and sweetness. If you wait beyond this point, the sugar of peas and corn will turn to starch, beans will become stringy, and beets woody. If possible, harvest early in the morning when the sugar content is highest. Before harvesting root crops, water the soil first so roots will come up without breaking.

For most vegetables, picking and tasting a few is the only sure test of readiness. Harvesting a crop too early not only prevents it from reaching full size but also often detracts from its developing full flavor. Harvesting too late may increase crop size but often at the expense of tenderness. Also, a vegetable left on the plant too long drains plant energy, causing a slow-down in production.

For processing, have all your equipment ready before you pick the vegetables; the quality can be greatly reduced by a delay of even an hour or two. Plunge the vegetables to be processed in cold water to cool them immediately after picking.

Be careful when canning vegetables with a high content of starch or protein—beans or corn, for example. Highly toxic organisms can develop in jars or cans if you cut short the sterilizing or cooking time or if you seal containers inadequately. Greens or acid vegetables, such as tomatoes, are comparatively less likely to spoil.

Cool storage. In cold-winter areas before severe frosts, you can prepare root crops, such as carrots, beets, turnips, rutabaga, and parsnips, for winter storage by digging the roots and removing the leaves. Dig cabbage, Brussels sprouts, and Chinese cabbage (roots and all) when the foliage is dry. Wet foliage can cause the whole pile to rot. Knock the soil off the roots; remove the outer leaves. Don't wash vegetables before storing them. Make a 6-inch layer of dry leaves or hay; lay the vegetables on it in a shallow layer. Mound leaves or hay 12 to 24 inches deep over the vegetables, covering them with a plastic sheet held down with soil. This insulation should prevent the vegetables from freezing until extremely cold weather arrives. Some gardeners utilize coldframes as root cellars for fall storage of heading or rooting vegetables, filling them with leaves as insulation.

Late-frost protection. Tomato, eggplant, and pepper plants will continue to ripen through late fall if you cover them with large clear plastic bags. These gather solar heat during the day and allow it to dissipate slowly during the night. Lightly covering plants with old blankets, tarps, or drop cloths offers even better protection on very cold nights.

Chinese cabbage, celery, endive, and cabbage can be protected in place from freezing by mounding leaves or straw over the plants and covering them lightly with soil to keep them in place and to reduce blowing. This will preserve vegetables through all but very severe freezes.

Rinsing soil *from vegetables in the garden, especially root crops, keeps dirt out of the kitchen.*

A Gardener's Guide to Vegetables

In this guide you will discover answers to such questions as which vegetables are the easiest to grow and which are the most difficult, which will deliver the fastest harvest and which the slowest, which are practically free of problems and which almost ask for trouble.

For quick reference, the major kinds of vegetables are listed in alphabetical order. Under each heading you will find recommendations for the best varieties to choose and specific directions for planting, watering, feeding, dealing with pests, harvesting, container use.

Artichokes

Large, bushy perennial. Set out plants or roots in early spring; harvest 'chokes the following spring.

Long, mild winters and cool summers are needed to produce the heavy vegetative growth that supports the large, edible flower buds of this delicacy. Highly decorative, massive plants have huge, deeply cut leaves. These well up into a silvery green fountain that can spread to 6 feet wide. Flower buds that escape harvest ripen into large, violet pink thistle blossoms that can be dried for arrangements and will last for several years.

Three or four established plants will provide plenty of artichoke buds for a small family.

Recommended variety. 'Green Globe' is usually the only variety available.

How to plant. You can grow artichokes from root divisions either purchased or separated from a desirable mother plant. Divide roots in autumn when foliage has died back. Expose a side shoot with a sharp spray of water. Cut it off 6 to 8 inches below the crown. Rangy plants with small, late-maturing buds may result if you start from seeds.

In early spring, root divisions are available in nurseries or garden supply stores and by mail order. In the West and along the Gulf and Southeastern coasts, you can plant the divisions any time after late winter.

Choose a spot that has well-drained, fertile soil and is warmed by full sun, except in very hot areas where artichokes appreciate afternoon shade. For each root division, dig a hole 18 inches deep and 4 to 5 feet apart. Fill the hole with water and let it soak in. For each plant, mix a bucketful of organic matter with some of the removed soil and partially refill the holes. Position the roots vertically, covering the old root with soil but leaving the base of the new, leafy shoots just above the soil line. Water again to settle the soil and complete filling the hole. Water every other day until new growth appears.

Care. Pull or hoe weeds or spread a straw mulch under the leaf canopy. Weeds steal water and nutrients from the plants. Every week or two during dry weather, let the hose trickle for an hour or two at the base of the plants.

Artichokes are heavy feeders and will respond to high nitrogen, water-soluble fertilizers applied every three to four weeks. Feed after a heavy watering. Follow the feeding with a light watering to dissolve and flush the fertilizer down into the root zone.

Pests. Aphids, earwigs, and worms sometimes get between the leaf bracts in the artichokes. If you think this has happened, right after picking immerse the artichokes for 10 minutes in warm salt water. The critters will crawl out. Give the buds a final upside-down shaking to force out the stubborn ones.

Harvesting. Each plant should bear a few buds the first season. From the second year on, plants should produce from 24 to 48 buds from late winter through midsummer. The harvest period will be earlier where winters are warm.

Cut the buds before the fleshy, edible bracts begin to open in preparation for flowering. Leave a 1½-inch length of stem on each bud when you cut it. After each major stem has completed fruiting, it will begin to dry up and can be removed. New, fruiting shoots will form throughout the season.

In containers. These handsome plants will thrive in containers with a soil capacity of at least 2 cubic feet.

Asparagus

One of the earliest vegetable crops. Set out plants or roots as early in the year as they're available. Wait two years for the first harvest.

The tasty spears of this hardy perennial push up from heavy root masses from early spring until warm weather arrives and occasionally through midsummer. (Asparagus needs a winter dormancy period to thrive.) Mature asparagus plants look completely unlike the spears; they reach from 4 to 6 feet in height and billow out to a width of 3 feet. These feathery, decorative plumes should be left on the plant until they have begun to dry in late autumn; they manufacture the food reserves that maintain strong crowns from year to year. Cut the stems to the ground only after the foliage turns brown.

Although asparagus takes several years to come into full production, the plants are very long lived—up to 20 years or more. Two dozen plants should yield enough spears for a small family.

Recommended varieties. 'U.C. 711', 'Mary Washington', 'California 500'.

How to plant. Since three years are required to produce spears from seed-grown plants, most gardeners prefer to start from roots. Roots are available during the late winter in Western states and can be planted as early as they are available. In other areas, mail order is the usual source. Plant the roots as soon as you receive them.

Asparagus plants need lots of room and full sun. Plant them at the back of the garden or along a fence where the tall foliage won't be in the way. Because the plants will be in place for many years, the soil should be broken up to a depth of 18 inches and large volumes of organic matter, such as well-rotted manure, should be worked in thoroughly. Don't skimp on the width of the bed; the prepared soil should extend 18 inches beyond the crowns. Mixing in organic matter should raise the bed 2 to 3 inches above the surrounding soil; this improves drainage.

For each crown, dig a hole 5 to 8 inches deep in the prepared bed and fill it with water. Pile a cone of loose soil 3 to 4 inches high in the center of the hole. Set the crown in the hole and spread out the fleshy roots. Fill the hole with soil and firm it down lightly around the roots. Water the crown again.

Care. Cultivate only in the top inch of the soil so you don't injure the network of roots. Pull weeds by hand before they get started in the bed, where they will be difficult to pull out without injuring the asparagus roots.

Perforated sprinkler hoses provide an excellent device for the deep watering needed by asparagus, since beds are too wide for basins or furrows. Let the sprinkler run for several hours every week or two during dry weather.

Feed with a complete fertilizer high in nitrogen when plants put on a growth spurt—usually around midsummer. When you remove the brown foliage in the fall, add a mulch of 2 to 3 inches of coarse organic matter, such as well-rotted manure. Do not use peat moss or leaves as a mulch; they form a crust or pack down, preventing moisture from penetrating the bed and hindering emerging spears.

Pests. The organic mulch over the beds makes a good hiding place for snails, slugs, sowbugs, and earwigs.

(Continued on next page)

Scatter meal or pellets of bait over the bed every two to three weeks to control them. Control asparagus beetles with sevin (following label precautions) after the cutting period. Don't spray after spears have poked their heads up, since they grow rapidly and will be cut within days.

Harvesting. Begin harvesting spears the second year after planting crowns or the third year after planting seeds. Harvest for two to three weeks or until the spears start appearing thinner. Then let them grow foliage for the rest of the season.

Cut spears when they are 6 to 8 inches high, at a point between the surface of the soil and 1½ inches deep, trying to avoid injury to the crowns or spears developing below the surface.

At the start of the cutting season, you will probably be able to harvest some spears every three days. As the soil warms, you may have to harvest daily. Spears taller than 8 inches have passed the best harvest stage, so let them develop foliage.

In containers. A wide-spreading root system makes asparagus a poor choice for container growing.

Beans

When the weather warms, beans will go from seed to table in 60 days. The biggest problem is deciding which of the many kinds to grow.

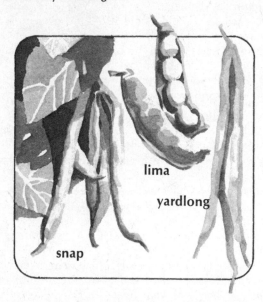

lima

yardlong

snap

Of the many types of beans, the two most frequently grown by home gardeners are snap beans and lima beans. Each of these can be divided into two kinds: low growing (bush beans) and tall growing (pole or runner beans). The legume family also contains many delicious vegetables that have beanlike seeds but that only remotely resemble the familiar types of beans. These in-

clude fava or broad beans, Southern peas, and asparagus or yardlong beans. The similarities in the culture of all of these beans are discussed first; then their individual characteristics are noted.

How to plant. Plant beans from seeds sown in the ground as soon as the soil has warmed up. Beans are frost tender and require a soil temperature of 65° to sprout reliably. Either check the soil temperature with a soil thermometer or wait until late-leafing trees—oaks, hickories, pecans—uncurl new spring foliage. Successive crops may be planted until midsummer.

Plant seeds of bush beans 3 inches apart in rows 18 inches apart. Pole bean plants are much larger, requiring 3 feet between rows and 9 to 12 inches between plants. If you want to run the vines up tepee-shaped supports, dig holes in the corners of a 3-foot square and plant three pole bean seeds in each. Cover seeds 1 inch deep in clay soils, 1½ inches in sandy soils.

Care. To avoid the spread of diseases from plant to plant, cultivate shallowly and only when the foliage is dry. Water frequently by soaking the soil instead of sprinkling—moist foliage invites bacterial diseases (in humid areas) and mildew.

High-nitrogen fertilizers and heavy applications of compost will encourage more foliage growth than vegetable production. Use a fertilizer with a nitrogen-phosphorus-potassium ratio of 1:2:2, applying it every three to four weeks in a shallow furrow about 6 inches away from the plants. Cover the fertilizer band with soil. If you furrow-irrigate, apply the fertilizer in the furrows so water can carry it into the root zone of the bean plants.

Pests. Birds will often pull seedlings out of the ground. Cover the rows with an arched arbor of chicken wire to protect the seedlings until they are 6 inches high.

Several little round beetles and their larvae as well as several kinds of moth larvae feed on bean foliage and pods. Pick beetles off plants (some are nocturnal—find them by flashlight). If that isn't successful, control them with rotenone or malathion. (Follow label precautions so you spray far enough away from the harvest date.)

Nematodes can also be a problem on beans. They are tiny, round worms that make swellings on the roots of plants. Try to keep them out of your garden by making sure that plants and soil brought into your garden are uninfested. If nematodes do appear, marigolds planted in the infested area have been found to deter them. Persistent infestations can be cured by treating the soil with fumigants *before* planting.

Harvesting. Pick bean pods when they are at least 3 inches long but before they begin to get tough and stringy. At the ideal point, beans should be just starting to bulge the sides. The more faithful you are about frequent picking, the longer the plants will yield. Pull the pods off carefully while holding the fruiting stems with your free hand. This prevents breaking off stems and destroying plants.

Tepee frame *made of 8-foot 1 by 1s and twine supports pole beans, creates a hideout.*

Slanted strings *make beans easy to pick; raised bed provides warm, rich, well-drained soil.*

In containers. Grow the bush forms of snap or lima beans, soybeans, or Southern peas in at least 8 to 12 inches of soil. For best results, add some garden soil to a commercial or homemade potting mix. The mix for soybeans should be especially fast draining.

SNAP BEANS

Often called string beans, these grow as self-supporting bushes or as climbing vines. The compact plant size, high productivity, and easy culture of bush beans make them one of the most popular of the summer vegetables. Runner or pole varieties require more work and attention because of the support needed by their long, twining vines, but they outyield bush varieties by a wide margin. Some pole varieties tend to be more flavorful than many bush types because, with bush beans, breeders have concentrated on good mechanical harvesting characteristics instead of flavor. Although certain bush and runner varieties mentioned below are grown for shelled beans, their young pods are also delicious.

Since bush beans require only six to seven weeks to mature in warm weather, they can be grown successfully in areas with fairly short summers. Pole beans need from 10 days to two weeks more than bush types to begin bearing.

Recommended varieties. Bush varieties are 'Green Crop', 'Tendercrop', 'Bush Romano', 'Bush Blue Lake', 'Tenderbest', 'Tenderette', 'Cherokee Wax', 'Honey Gold', 'Dwarf Horticultural' (shell bean). Pole or runner varieties are 'Blue Lake', 'Kentucky Wonder', 'Romano' or 'Italian', 'Royalty' (purple), 'Burpee Golden', 'Oregon Giant' (shell bean).

LIMA BEANS

Both the bush and pole types of lima beans have larger and more spreading vines than their snap bean counterparts. Because they also mature three to five weeks later and require warmer soil to sprout reliably, lima beans are most successfully grown in areas where summers are long and rather warm.

Limas are planted much like snap beans except they need more space—plant them 4 to 6 inches apart in a row. In clay soils, plant seeds on edge to improve the chances of germination. Limas prefer a lean soil and should be fertilized sparingly. Too much nitrogen results in heavy vine growth and few pods.

Pick the pods as soon as they begin to look a little lumpy from the swelling of seeds and before they begin to turn yellow. Keeping pods picked will prolong production. You can store sun-dried seeds for several months in sealed jars.

(Continued on next page)

Small-seeded baby limas or "butterbeans" are traditionally preferred in the Southeast. Plump-seeded "potato" limas are usually grown in other parts of the country.

Recommended varieties. Butterbeans: 'Henderson Bush','Jackson Wonder Bush' (speckled), 'Florida Butter Pole' (speckled), 'Small White' or 'Sieva Pole'. Potato limas: 'Fordhook 242 Bush', 'Dixie Butterpea Bush', 'Christmas Pole' (speckled), 'King of the Garden Pole'.

ASPARAGUS OR YARDLONG BEANS

This species is used in Oriental cooking. The plants, with their long runners and bean pods that reach 18 to 24 inches in length, somewhat resemble Southern peas. A long, warm season is required to mature this bean.

DRY BEANS

Culture is the same as for the bush type of snap beans. Let the beans remain on the bush until the pods turn dry or begin to shatter. Thresh them from their hulls and thoroughly dry them before storing for later use. Varieties include 'Pinto', 'Red Kidney', 'Great Northern', and 'White Marrowfat'.

SOYBEANS

The green seeds are shelled from the short, plump, furry pods and cooked for their high protein and oil content. Soybeans grow best in the warm, humid South and Midwest and do poorly in most dry climates. Grow them much as you would bush lima beans; the bushes are about the same size.

BROAD BEANS OR FAVA BEANS

The name comes from the long, rather broad, flattened green pods that are shelled to produce large, meaty seeds. They require long periods of cool weather to mature. Plant them in late summer or fall in mild-winter climates and in very early spring elsewhere. The plants grow 3 to 4½ feet high.

SOUTHERN PEAS OR COWPEAS

Although referred to as "peas" in the Southern states, these plants more closely approximate beans in appearance and cultural requirements. Tropical in origin, Southern peas need about four months of warm days and nights to set good crops of pods.

Generally available varieties, such as 'Blackeye', 'Purple Hull', and 'Crowder', have large, spreading plants, 2 feet or more in height. Newer varieties mature earlier and have more compact plants.

Harvest and shell peas before the pods turn yellow or let overly mature pods dry and shell the seeds for winter storage.

FLAGEOLETS

Popular in France, flageolets have a creamy texture and mellow flavor when they're shelled, simmered in water for about 1½ hours, and served with butter. Plant seeds in spring (after the soil has warmed up) in rich soil an inch deep and 3 inches apart in rows 2½ feet apart. Make furrows before planting for deep watering.

Beets

Plant seeds from spring through fall as long as the weather is cool. Use roots and tops in 6-8 weeks.

Beets are a little slow to sprout from their corky seeds but, once started, grow rapidly and produce a great deal of delicious food in a small amount of space. They attract few pests and tolerate warm but prefer cool weather. (Where summers are very hot, plant beets to mature before and after hot weather.) You can eat both the roots and the immature tops.

You can grow winter crops of beets in mild climates; seeds should be sown in early fall and the roots harvested before they begin to shoot up seed stalks the following spring.

Recommended varieties. 'Detroit Dark Red', 'Ruby Queen', 'Firechief', 'Formanova' (large and cylindrical roots), 'Burpee's Golden', 'Green Top Bunching' (beautiful green leaves).

How to plant. To maintain a supply of beets throughout the summer, plant seeds in short rows as early as the soil can be worked in the spring and at monthly intervals until late summer. Cover seeds with ¼ inch of sand, vermiculite, or finely pulverized compost to improve germination. Sow seeds 1 inch apart. Thin to at least 2 inches apart when plants are small, using the greens of the pulled plants.

Care. Beets need frequent watering in dry weather to keep the roots tender and plump.

Light applications of a complete fertilizer every three to four weeks will help the roots form quickly and remain tender.

Pests. Beets interest few pests except a kind of grub called a root maggot and slugs that can burrow into roots or spoil the tops of small plants. Root maggots can be discouraged by digging in heavy applications of compost and by not planting root crops in the same location each year. Look for slugs and hand pick them when you find them.

Harvesting. Begin pulling beets to eat as soon as they reach 1 inch in diameter; this will make room for the remaining roots to grow to their mature size of 2 to 3 inches in diameter. When beets are tiny, both tops and roots can be cooked together. Don't let beets grow to jumbo sizes; they can develop streaks of woody tissue.

In containers. Beets will thrive in planter boxes deep enough for their roots (about 12 inches). Give them 3 inches between plants.

Harvest broccoli *head with some leaves. Buds below cut will form heads for later picking.*

Broccoli

Hardy cabbage relative. Start plants to mature during cool weather but before severe frosts.

This cool-season crop bears over a long season. The leafy, erect plants reach from 1½-2 feet tall. Broccoli has been much improved in recent years through the efforts of plant breeders developing better varieties for commercial freezing. They increased the size and holding ability of the central head and reduced plant size.

Frost-hardy broccoli plants should be transplanted to the garden in early spring to mature ahead of hot days or in early fall so they will be ready for harvest before killing frost. In mild Western climates, winter broccoli can be grown successfully, but plants should begin to head before the onset of cold weather.

Recommended varieties. 'Green Comet' and 'Neptune' are good hybrids. 'Green Mountain', 'Waltham 29', 'De Cicco', and 'Calabrese' are older varieties but yield well. 'De Rapa' is one of the original Italian sprouting types that does not form large central heads.

How to plant. Grow spring broccoli from started plants; start fall or winter broccoli from seeds sown in the garden in late summer. Where summers aren't too warm, sow seed in the garden in early spring. Sow seeds ½ inch deep and 1 inch apart. Later transplant to 2½ to 3 feet apart. Spring broccoli will mature in 50-60 days; winter crops need 75-90 days to form heads.

Care. Give broccoli plenty of water and push it along with frequent applications of high-nitrogen plant food to develop the big, vigorous plants that are necessary to support large heads. Plant short rows; six plants are sufficient to feed four people. To avoid having many heads maturing at once, plant three plants at three-week intervals.

Pests. Broccoli heads are so large and tight that cabbage worms and aphids can be difficult to eliminate. Try hosing off aphids or using a soapy solution on them (see page 54). If you use malathion, spray before heads form and follow label precautions. Control cabbage worms with a spray of the biological insecticide *Bacillus thuringiensis.*

(Continued on next page)

Harvesting. Cut the central heads while the buds are still tight. Include up to 6 inches of the edible stem and leaves. Pierce the lower stem with your thumbnail; peel off and discard the skin where it is hard and woody. Broccoli will send up edible shoots after you harvest the central head. Keeping shoots harvested before flowering will encourage production as long as the weather is cool. When the weather warms, the heat will force broccoli to flower—then it's past the good-eating stage.

In containers. Large plants make broccoli impractical for containers.

Brussels sprouts

A plant set out in spring or fall can provide a hundred tiny sprouts as long as the weather stays cool.

This member of the cabbage family produces edible "sprouts" that look like tiny cabbages. Not everyone can grow sprouts because of their preference for a long growing period of cool weather. The plants grow large and the sprouts cluster tightly around the tall main stem, maturing from the base up. Harvesting can continue for many weeks. Four to six plants can feed four people.

Recommended varieties. 'Long Island Improved' is an old favorite; 'Jade Cross Hybrid' is a heavy producer and can be started early enough for short-season areas.

How to plant. Where summers are short but cool, purchase plants early and transplant them to the garden as soon as the soil can be worked in the spring. Protect plants on very cold nights by placing wide-mouth glass jars over them. Remove these during the day so the plants don't cook. (Light frosts won't harm the plants.)

Four to five months of cool weather are required for Brussels sprouts to mature from seeds. In California's

coastal belt, start seeds in the garden in late summer; elsewhere set out plants so the sprouts will mature during cool weather. Plant seeds $1/2$ inch deep. Transplant to stand $2^1/2$ to 3 feet apart.

Care. Give sprouts ample water and encourage growth with frequent applications of a high-nitrogen fertilizer. Remove leaves from all but the top of the plant as sprouts crowd them.

Pests. Try to keep aphids hosed off before they get inside the sprouts.

Harvesting. Snap or trim off the sprouts when they are firm and still deep green; they are at their best when about 1 to $1^1/2$ inches in diameter. A well-grown plant can yield 75 to 100 sprouts over a 30 to 45 day period. Mild frosts improve their flavor, but where winters are severe, the harvest can be prolonged by uprooting the plants with a spade, snapping off the leaves, laying the plants on a bed of straw or leaves, covering the roots with soil, and spreading 6 to 12 inches of straw or leaves over the plants to insulate them.

In containers. Large plant requires a massive container, but high yield makes growing one plant worthwhile.

Cabbage

Space-eater, pests love it, but delicious, abundant crops reward you in cool weather.

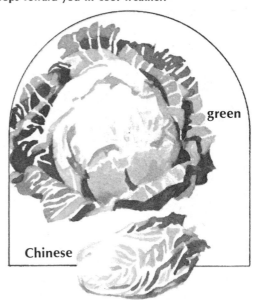

green

Chinese

If you have judged cabbage by the pale, often strong-tasting heads sold commercially, you will be surprised to discover the delicious flavor of the vegetable when home grown, as well as the variety of rich colors and leaf textures available. You can choose from among several red varieties and the crinkly leafed "savoy" varieties, in addition to the green cabbages.

Cabbage should be planted to mature during cool weather. You can grow spring and fall crops where the cool but frost-free growing season is five months or more in length. Plant early varieties or hybrids in the spring; these mature in 7 to 8 weeks from transplants. Later varieties, such as the king-size kraut cabbage, need up to 12 weeks to mature from seeds and should be planted after midsummer for fall harvest. Winter cabbage can be grown in mild-climate areas, but the heads tend to burst and send up flower stalks as a result of warm spells.

Recommended varieties. Early miniatures are 'Dwarf Morden', 'Earliana'. Early to midseason varieties are 'Resistant Golden Acre', 'Early Jersey Wakefield', 'Emerald Cross', 'Harvester Queen', 'Greenback', 'King Cole', 'Salad Green' (for cole slaw). Red types are 'Red Head' and 'Ruby Bell'; late-maturing varieties are 'Premium Flat Dutch', 'Savoy Chieftain'.

How to plant. Plant cabbage in a different spot every year to avoid pests. Spring cabbage is usually grown from plants to gain three to four weeks time. Grow fall cabbage from seeds sown in the garden after midsummer. When buying spring cabbage plants, look for a light purple cast to the leaves. This indicates that they have been properly hardened-off.

Plant seeds ½ inch deep. Transplant them 24 to 30 inches apart. Make sure to set in the plants to the same depth that they grew in the flat and to firm the soil around the roots.

Care. Grow cabbage rapidly with frequent light applications of high-nitrogen fertilizer and regular watering. Cabbage responds favorably to the cool, moist soil conditions produced by a mulch of hay or straw.

Pests. Aphids are prevalent and persistent pests. Control them with a soapy water spray (see page 54) or use rotenone or malathion (note label precautions).

The most serious pest of the cabbage is the green cabbage worm, the larva of a small, white butterfly often found hovering over cabbage patches in late spring. Cabbage worm feeds on the tender young leaves, producing ragged holes, and often burrows into the heads. Good control can be achieved by using one of the dusts or sprays for chewing insects; *Bacillus thuringiensis* and rotenone are effective.

You can control cabbage root maggot, a small, yellowish white maggot that tunnels into the roots and causes plants to wilt, by spraying the ground around young seedlings with diazinon.

Harvesting. Begin harvesting heads when they are firm and about the size of a softball. Cut just beneath the head, leaving some basal leaves to support new growth of small lateral heads. (See Brussels sprouts for directions for storing heads.) A light frost won't hurt them, but don't allow the heads to freeze before harvest.

In containers. Deep roots and large heads make most cabbage impractical for containers. Exceptions are flow-

Cabbage seedling *with six-week head start demonstrates the ideal transplanting size.*

ering and miniature forms or Chinese cabbage harvested while young for salad greens.

CHINESE CABBAGE

The main secret to successful culture of this delicious vegetable is the planting date. Except for some hybrids, Chinese cabbage quickly shoots up flower heads during the long days of summer, so spring plantings are risky except in the cool northern tier of states or along the Western coast fog belt. Elsewhere, delay planting until after midsummer, when the shortening days and cool weather will permit heads to grow to a large size before extremely cold weather freezes them. Chinese cabbage matures in 65 to 80 days from seeds sown directly in the garden.

Plant seeds ½ inch deep in garden rows. Eat the excess seedlings and let the remainder stand 12 to 18 inches apart. Fertilize and water frequently to sustain rapid growth. Pests are few except for the wormlike cabbage loopers; spray with *Bacillus thuringiensis* (note label precautions).

Heads can be protected for several weeks against freezing by lifting the outer leaves and mounding soil up around the heads.

Recommended varieties. 'Michihli' has long, slender, tapering heads. 'Wong Bok' is short and barrel-shaped, very desirable because of their high proportion of green leaf area to white stem.

Carrots

Two secrets to success with carrots: keep seeds moist until they're up; provide loose soil for long roots.

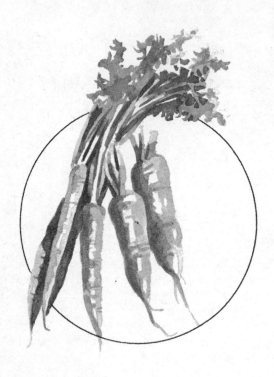

Few other vegetables can match home-grown carrots for vitamin content and sweet flavor. Carrots have the happy habit of remaining in good condition long after maturity, so roots are rarely wasted. And even though carrots prefer cool weather, crops can be grown in mid-summer in all areas of the country but the South. In mild-winter areas, if you plant carrots in early fall, the roots will continue to grow slowly during the winter, insuring a steady supply for salads, stews, and carrot sticks. Most varieties require 65 to 75 days to grow to full size.

Recommended varieties. 'Nantes' and 'Goldinhart' are very sweet and tender and of medium length. The miniature 'Tiny Sweet' is just the right size for finger carrots. 'Red-Cored Chantenay' has heavy, stumpy roots and excels in shallow soils. 'Gold Pak' needs deep topsoil for its long roots to develop.

How to plant. From the size of the mature carrot root, you could guess that they would need deep, porous soil to develop to full size. Adding a thin layer of topsoil won't do; you have to open up the hard clay or silt soils to a 1-foot depth by spading in organic matter, such as well-rotted manure or peat moss. Too much coarse compost, however, will cause carrot roots to

fork. Minimize soil compaction by laying boards between rows to walk on. Or try the sand trench method by planting seeds ½ inch deep in a trench of sand 2 inches wide and 8 inches deep. Feeder roots will grow sideways through the sand and draw nutrients from the soil.

Plant seeds ½ inch deep and ½ inch apart; later thin to 2 inches and finally to 3 inches as you remove half-grown roots for kitchen use. Germination can fail in dry weather when the soil dries out quickly and crusts form. You can improve sprouting by covering the seeded furrow with a board or plastic sheet as explained on page 37. Seedlings look almost grasslike when the first leaves emerge, so weed carefully.

Starting carrot seeds in pots and transplanting them to the garden has some advantages over sowing seeds directly in the ground. Because germination is more certain in pots, you save on seeds. You also save the labor of early weeding and thinning. Still another advantage: you can sow at any time of the year.

Sow 10 to 12 seeds evenly in a 4 or 6 inch pot. Keep the soil damp, thinning to six or eight evenly spaced carrots per pot. Set out by planting the entire clump in the planting hole, turning it out of the pot carefully to avoid breaking the soil ball. Harvest the whole clump at once.

Care. Carrots respond to frequent light applications of fertilizer and regular watering by developing large and tender roots. Rough roots can result from prolonged wet, cool weather. Twisted, distorted roots are often caused by delaying thinning too long. Forking and branching roots result from the use of fresh manure, rough, slow-decaying compost, or layers of hard soil. And infrequent watering can cause cracking of roots; the hard roots can literally swell and burst open when they finally get water.

Pests. Carrot rust fly is the one enemy which can be considered serious. Its larvae tunnel into roots of carrots. This is primarily a warm-weather pest; plant carrots to mature in cool weather so grubs won't disfigure them. Or try digging in lots of well-rotted compost to encourage natural predators.

Harvesting. Begin pulling carrots as soon as roots reach finger size, harvesting all roots before seed heads form. If the soil is a little hard, prying roots with a trowel as you pull up on the tops will prevent them from breaking off; or water before pulling. If you do break off a top, dig out and eat the root; it may not grow a new top.

Carrot roots are easy to store where winters are severe (elsewhere, leave them in the ground). Before the soil freezes, dig the roots, break off the heavy part of the tops, and store the roots in dry sand or in leaf or straw pits or piles, as described on page 55.

In containers. Short varieties and miniatures are best choices. Soil should be at least 12 inches deep and very loose.

Cauliflower

Late summer is a good time to set out plants in most areas. Harvest in 2-3 months.

A cool-weather crop grown for early summer and fall harvest, cauliflower will flower rapidly if the weather turns hot. Winter harvests are possible in mild Western or Gulf Coast climates. Plants are fairly frost hardy. Allow 60 to 80 days from transplanting to harvest—90 to 100 days for winter crops. See broccoli for culture, care, and pest control.

Start cauliflower from small plants set out 18 to 20 inches apart in rows 20 inches apart. Keep plants actively growing; any growth check might cause premature setting of undersized heads.

Unlike broccoli, with its erect plants, cauliflower forms its edible buds only a few inches above the ground. Blanching of heads whitens them by excluding light and can be done simply by gathering the long wrapper leaves and securing them at the top with a wide rubber band. This prevents the formation of green or purplish pigment. Unwrap the heads occasionally to check for pests.

If the weather does turn hot, an overhead sprinkling will create the humidity that cauliflower needs. But don't substitute this for deep soaking.

Harvest heads before the bud segments or "curds" begin to separate in preparation for shooting up flower heads.

Recommended varieties. 'Snowball' and 'Snow King hybrid.' 'Purple Head' has large plants with heads of a deep purple color that turn green in cooking and a flavor somewhat like broccoli. It needs no blanching.

In containers. Large size of each plant makes cauliflower impractical in containers.

Celery

Well-developed stalks demand rich soil, ample water and nutrients, and a long, cool season. Slow-growing crop; buying plants speeds results.

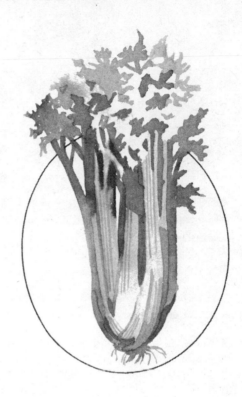

If your area enjoys about four months of cool weather and if you can provide a deep bed of sandy or organic soil, you can grow celery rather easily. Elsewhere you may end up with tough stalks on plants that go to seed. Instead of being a total loss, however, leaves, stalks, and seeds all make good flavoring.

Recommended varieties. 'Giant Pascal' and 'Tall Utah' seeds and plants are generally available; 'Slow Bolt' is used where early spring-planted celery is subjected to light frosts. A self-blanching variety, 'Golden Detroit', has pale gold stalks.

Celeriac—a close relative—is grown like celery. It forms rough, knobby, rounded roots that are peeled and used in soups and stews. Since plants are seldom available, grow celeriac from seeds.

How to plant. In hot climates, best results come from seeds or transplants started in late summer. In mild West Coast areas you can grow celery almost year round. If you're in doubt about your winter's effect, try glass or plastic frost protectors (see pages 38-39); or start seeds indoors in January and set out seedlings in early spring.

If you use seeds, soak them first. They germinate in about 10 days, are ready to transplant into the ground

Celery transplant *goes into richly prepared planting bed. Harvest in about four months.*

Chard

All the same uses as spinach but not as fussy about weather or soil. Plant seeds in spring and summer.

when they are about 3 inches high, in 10 to 12 weeks. Sometimes nurseries sell seedlings in 2-inch pots or six-packs.

Work in plenty of fertilizer and soil conditioners before transplanting celery into the ground. Space plants about 6 inches apart. Stagger the harvest period by transplanting only a half dozen or so at one time. Make furrows between rows and irrigate thoroughly and often. (If plants dry out, they get tough.)

Care. When plants are about half mature size (about 2½ months after transplanting), begin forcing them to grow rapidly. Feed and water frequently.

Pests. Celery worm, the colorful larva of the black swallowtail butterfly, may feed on celery foliage. If they do serious damage, remove them by hand or spray with *Bacillus thuringiensis*.

Harvesting. Some gardeners harvest a few stalks at a time as soon as they look ready; others wait until the plant forms a tight head, then cut off the whole thing just above the roots. New stalks grow from the roots; they are smaller and less succulent than the first stalks.

Surplus fall-crop heads can be stored for weeks if dug up, roots and all, before frost and kept in a well-ventilated, cool place. Or heads can be protected in place by piling straw against them and holding it down with soil.

In containers. Although celery can succeed in deep containers, plants need even more watering and feeding than they do in the ground. This results in a great deal of maintenance over a long growing period.

Few vegetables can match Swiss chard for ease of growth and heavy, extended production of delicious, crinkly green leaves and wide, crisp stems. Six to eight plants can feed a family for several months because new center leaves continually replace the large outer leaves as they are harvested.

A member of the beet family, chard can be harvested 60 days following spring planting or 45 days after summer planting. Plants withstand summer heat in most areas, yet will mature by midsummer where summers are cool.

Recommended varieties. 'Fordhook Giant', 'Lucullus', 'White Ribbed'. 'Rhubarb' chard has red stems and ribs and dark green leaves. It is decorative enough to be used in groups among flowers.

How to plant. Grow chard from seeds sown outdoors as soon as the soil can be worked in the spring. In mild-winter areas, chard can be planted any time of the year, but fall plantings shoot to seed the following spring. Plant seeds ½ inch deep and 1 inch apart. Thin plants to 8 to 12 inches apart; eat the excess plants. Chard seeds are well adapted to band planting or broadcasting.

Care. Feed chard every two to three weeks and water frequently. The plants may wilt slightly on hot days but will recover quickly if the soil around them is soaked.

Pests. Chard is virtually pest-free. If aphids attack the plants, blast them off with a fine, sharp spray of water.

Harvesting. Harvest the outer leaves as needed and before the stems get stringy. Break or cut them off at the base. Replacement leaves will grow from the center. Always leave a few center leaves so the plants can manufacture sugars to sustain themselves.

In containers. No other vegetable can match chard for sustained heavy yield from a small space. Use containers with a soil depth of 12-24 inches. If you remove the outer leaves to use, the plant will continue to grow.

Chayote

If you like the flavor of this unusual fruit and live in a mild-winter area, plant a few of the fruits you buy and you'll have a lush, prolific vine for many summers.

Plant whole chayote, *slanted, with sprouted end down, the other end barely covered.*

This perennial member of the squash family from the tropics can be eaten raw or cooked like squash. Fruits are usually pale green, oval, smooth-skinned, and furrowed; but some plants produce fruit that's darker green, round, or spiny. The vines climb tall by tendrils —sometimes to 50 feet. The tops of the vine will die back in winter, but the roots send up new growth each spring for many years. This is a plant for mild winter climates. Cold weather slows growth and production and frost kills plants to the ground.

How to plant. Buy the fruit in the winter for planting and store in a cool place (the refrigerator is too cold) until the soil warms up in the spring. Plant the whole fruit (at least two for cross-pollination) slanted in the planting hole, with the seed end down and the small end exposed (see photo). If the fruits have sprouted before planting, cut back the shoots to 1 or 2 inches at planting time. If they haven't sprouted, the broadest end will usually show the seed tip peeping out of the fruit. Barely cover fruit, or leave stem end barely exposed. The planting site should be in the sun and in well-drained soil.

Care. Be careful not to overwater at first; overwatering causes the fruit to rot. Once the vine starts to grow, it needs occasional fertilizer and ample water. Commercial growers use well-rotted manure in the planting mix supplemented with additional high-nitrogen fertilizer.

Harvesting. Plants begin to bloom when days start to grow short—usually in late August. First fruits are ready for harvest about a month after bloom begins. In warm weather, plants may bear through December and January and produce as many as 50 to 100 fruits to the vine.

In containers. You can start chayotes in containers placed next to a fence or other large support, but growth is so rampant that roots will escape from the pots into the ground.

Collards

Plant seeds of this "headless cabbage" for cool-weather maturity. Flavor is improved by light frosts.

Grown all over the country for its succulent greens or leaves, this cabbage relative is most popular in the South, where it's summer planted for fall and winter harvest. The mature plants are frost hardy and yield sweet leaves after cold weather has concentrated their sugars.

Collards look like lanky, open-growing, nonheading cabbages. The plants can reach 2 to 3 feet in height. Although collards bear a superficial resemblance to their close relative, kale, their flavor is distinctly unique.

Recommended varieties. 'Vates' is a compact variety; 'Georgia' forms large plants.

How to plant. In areas with short, cool summers, plant seeds outdoors in late spring. Elsewhere, plant after midsummer. Sow seeds ½ inch deep and 1 inch apart. Thin to 18 to 24 inches apart; eat thinnings for greens.

Care. Keep the stems and leaves tender by watering and feeding frequently. The large leaves evaporate a lot of water, so soak the soil deeply. Feed every three to four weeks with a high-nitrogen fertilizer.

Pests. Collards have the same pests as cabbage; use the same controls.

Harvesting. Don't harvest the first six to eight leaves on the plants; let them develop to full size to sustain the plants. Clip off and cook younger leaves, including the stems, when they are about the size of your hand. If you harvest larger, older leaves, discard the stringy stems and test the leaf midrib for tenderness to see if it should be saved. Never harvest the central growing point or you will delay the production of new leaves until side shoots are formed.

In containers. Plants are large but will yield a continuous supply of greens in large tubs or deep boxes.

Corn

You need warm weather and a soil area big enough for at least three rows.

If garden-fresh sweet corn tastes better to you than the "store-bought" kind, you're not just imagining it. Unless corn ears are cooled to remove field heat immediately after harvesting, they begin at once to lose sugar.

Corn is a heat-loving vegetable. Untreated seeds won't sprout reliably until the soil reaches 60 to 65°. Extra-early hybrids (small plants with rather small ears) mature in about 60 days. The second-early or midseason maincrop hybrids mature in 65 to 80 days and have medium-sized to rather large ears and plants that reach 6 feet or more in height. Late varieties and hybrids require 90 days or more to harvest; most are tall plants.

Recommended varieties. Open-pollinated and non-hybrid varieties mature later, bear smaller ears, and show less disease resistance than most hybrids. Hybrids are selected not only for high row count and long ears but also for depth of kernels. Generally, the later the hybrid matures, the larger and longer the ears and deeper the kernels.

Hybrids are available with golden, white, and bi-colored ears. Each type has a distinct flavor. All are good but the "super sweet" hybrids are superior. Unless your growing season is very short, don't rely on the extra-early hybrids for your main crop, because they are low yielding. Don't plant late varieties if you live in an area where summers are short. Don't plant the super-sweet or extra-sweet hybrids near any other corn, or crossing will spoil the flavor. Popcorn, too, needs a separation of at least 300 feet from sweet corn.

Early Hybrids are 'Polar Vee', 'Early Sunglow', 'Early Xtra Sweet', 'Morning Sun', 'Golden Beauty', 'Golden Midget' (tiny ears), 'Seneca 60'. Midseason hybrids are 'Butter & Sugar' (bicolor), 'Super Sweet', 'FM Cross', 'Golden Cross Bantam', 'Golden Jubilee'. Late hybrids are 'Illini Xtra Sweet', 'Seneca Chief', 'Silver Queen' (white), 'Stylepak' (good for canning and freezing).

How to plant. Corn should be planted in a block of at least three rows (rather than in one row) to insure pollination. Corn pollen from the tassels must fall on the silks of the ears before kernels (seeds) will form. Wet or very hot weather can interfere with pollination. Missing kernels or poorly filled out ears can result from poor pollination or nutrient deficiencies. Providing you have the room, you can keep a constant supply of corn coming from midsummer until fall either by planting small blocks of one to two dozen plants every two weeks or by mixing seeds of hybrids of various maturity dates. Follow the latter course only if you plant a large block of at least three or four dozen plants to minimize pollination problems.

In climates where rain comes in the summer, gardeners generally plant rows or hills (see page 34) on flat ground and supply water with sprinklers if and when it's needed. But in dry-summer climates, it's best to prepare for a summer of heavy watering by building irrigation furrows at planting time (see page 34).

Use strings to line up straight rows in moist spaded or tilled ground, scoop out a trench, and pile soil along the rim of the trench. Space rows 30 to 36 inches apart. Plant seeds 4 to 6 inches apart.

Use your fingers or a trowel to bury seeds 1 to 2 inches deep in the shoulder of the excavated soil. Make sure you place the seed well down into moist soil. The seeds should sprout in four to seven days.

Unless it's very hot, seedlings usually won't need water until they grow 3 or 4 inches tall. As soon as soil around the seeds begins to dry out to a depth of 2 or 3 inches, fill furrows with water. Don't let seedlings wilt.

In dry-summer climates, water is the most important part of growing. After seedlings are up and growing vigorously, it's difficult to give them too much water, and dangerous to give them too little. In places where summers are rainy or cool, you may not have to water at all or only once or twice during the season.

Don't worry if corn leaves wilt in the hot part of the day; the root system isn't efficient enough to send wa-

Ripe corn has dry, brown silks (left), spurts milky juice at sweetest, most tender stage (right).

ter (even if plenty is there) up to the top of the plant. However, you should water right away if the plant has not recovered its freshness the next morning.

Care. When seedlings reach about 6 inches tall, give them more room by thinning them to stand 8 to 12 inches apart (closer for the more compact varieties).

Corn needs a good amount of fertilizer. Mixing in compost, manure, or fertilizer before planting may be enough, but in addition to, or in place of that, you generally should feed once during the season. Scatter complete fertilizer in furrows and water it in or apply liquid food in the furrows. Feed anytime between when the plants are 12 inches tall and when tassels form.

Weeds compete with young corn but usually get shaded out as the stalks grow tall. Shallowly hoe weeds every week for the first six or eight weeks. At the same time, scrape loose soil onto the hills around the plants.

Pests. Corn earworm is the worst corn pest. The adult moth lays eggs on the silks and the eggs hatch into worms that crawl into the ear to eat the kernels.

One way to reduce worm damage is to cut off the silks about three days after the ears reach full size. If you cut the silks off too soon, you'll get ears with kernels missing.

Another way to reduce earworm damage: using a medicine dropper, put 1/4 teaspoon of mineral oil on the silks of each ear after pollination. The oil smothers earworm eggs.

Harvesting. Timing is critical because the sugar in the kernels turns to starch as soon as the ear is picked or reaches a certain age. In warm weather, corn will be ready to eat about three weeks after you see the yellow pollen flying. When the silks dry up, slit the shucks and inspect the kernels for harvest readiness. They should be large and well colored but not tough when tested with your thumbnail. Milky juice spurts out if the ear is at the best eating stage. Clear juice means wait a few days. If the juice looks like toothpaste, you're too late.

Pop the harvested ears into ice water if you can't cook, freeze, or can them immediately. This will slow the conversion from sugar to starch. If you slip and let kernels get past the juicy "milk" and into the drier "dough" stage, you can still add milk and use the kernels for creamed corn.

In containers. Midget varieties yield best results in containers. Several tubs with at least three plants each will insure good pollination. Stalks require regular feeding and watering to set ears.

Cress

Flavor resembles watercress. Easy to grow as long as the weather is cool. Sow seeds in early spring.

In this salad-minded era, cress should not be overlooked as a nippy garnish. Upland or curly cress (small, parsley-like plants) grows easily and rapidly from seeds sown outdoors in cool weather. Watercress prefers wet feet and will thrive along a stream or pond bank where the water remains cool. Sow the seeds about 6 inches above the water line. Watercress can also be grown in pots of soil partly submerged in a large container of water after the seeds have sprouted indoors or outdoors.

In containers. Try growing cress indoors in a shallow tray. Sprinkle seeds on wet cheesecloth that has been spread on top of potting mix. Keep the cheesecloth moist and sticking to the soil surface. Snip seedlings to use in 10 to 14 days.

Cucumbers

As big as blackjacks or as small as your little finger; shaped like baby blimps, fat cigars, or even lemons; smooth or "warty"; for slicing or pickling—all grow fast in warm weather.

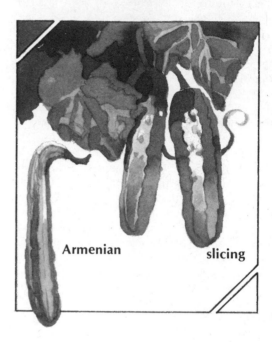

Armenian   slicing

If you like to fill shelves with jars of garden vegetables for winter use, plant cucumbers. Six to twelve vines will keep you busy pickling for several weeks. The vines of most varieties will spread over 6 feet before the plants are worn out from heavy bearing. Standard vining cucumbers are not for the small garden unless you can train them up supports.

Each cucumber vine bears both male and female flowers; female blossoms are recognizable by the swollen ovary just behind the flower. Pollen is transferred from male flowers by insects and wind. Certain hybrids have been selected for their high percentage of female flowers; seedsmen will usually mix in a few seeds of a male pollinator variety to insure fruiting. Fruits won't set without pollination; poorly formed fruits are usually caused by nutritional problems, too little or too much water, or hot weather.

Recommended varieties. Slicing varieties grow 6 to 9 inches in length. Young fruits can be pickled whole or the mature cucumbers sliced crosswise or into sticks for ease of packing into jars. 'Burpee Hybrid', 'Palomar', and 'Victory' are disease resistant. 'Burpless' and 'Armenian', oriental types, are reputedly easy to digest. Both have long, ribbed fruit; 'Armenian' is light green.

Pickling varieties have short, blocky fruits which are slightly more prolific than the slicers and are more con-

Four vines of Armenian cucumber wind around 8 by 8 post; gardener ties new growth to dowels.

Circle fence makes cucumbers accessible from all sides, saves space, keeps fruit off ground.

venient for making whole pickles. 'Bravo' and 'Chero-kee' hybrids are bred for the Southeast. 'Crispy' and 'Spartan Valor' hybrids are disease resistant. 'Lemon' has round, creamy yellow fruits and a unique flavor.

The new compact hybrids for small gardens, hanging baskets, and container growing include 'Little Minnie', 'Tiny Dill', and the early, disease-resistant 'Patio Pick'.

How to plant. Cucumbers are definitely a warm-weather vegetable. The seeds need warm soil to sprout, and the plants need warm weather to help pollination. (Pollination can be inhibited, though, by extreme dryness combined with heat.)

Plant the seeds 1 inch deep and 2 to 3 inches apart in a row and later thin to 12 inches apart. Closer spacing can increase yields, especially if you create a rich, fast-draining soil by incorporating lots of organic matter and if you mulch under the vines with straw.

If you expect some cool spells during the growing season, plant the seeds along fences where reflected heat will encourage faster growth and better fruiting. You can also start seeds indoors in peat pots two to three weeks before the usual date of the last spring frost.

Care. Cucumbers need lots of water. Sprinkling is not recommended for most gardens because it encourages mildew. Furrow irrigation works best but vines can clog the furrows. Train all the vines in one direction to keep the irrigation furrow open. In small gardens, train the vines up 3 to 5-foot-high vertical or slanted frames covered with chicken wire or strung with stout twine. Cucumber vines don't cling; tie them up every foot or so. Pinch out the tips of rambling vines; this will cause more branches to form. Feed every three to four weeks by scattering a complete fertilizer in the irrigation furrow and watering deeply.

Pests. Cucumber beetles feed on the leaves and can spread bacterial wilt, a fatal cucumber disease for which there is no known cure. The larva of the beetle also does damage, boring into the roots. Dust with diazinon or sevin. (Dusts are preferable to sprays, since moisture can cause mildew on cucumber plants). Cucumber beetle will usually show up only while plants are young.

Harvesting. With most varieties, pick for sweet pickles when 2 or 3 inches long, for dills when 5 or 6 inches, for slicing when 6 to 8 inches. Pick cucumbers before they begin to turn yellow, because at the yellow stage the seeds begin to harden. Keep fruits picked—leaving older fruits on vines inhibits the formation of new fruit. Hold the brittle vines firmly while twisting or clipping off the fruits to prevent breakage.

In containers. Try compact varieties, such as 'Little Minnie', 'Tiny Dill', and 'Patio Pick', in good-sized tubs or barrels. Include plenty of well-rotted manure or compost in the potting mix and feed plants frequently.

ARMENIAN CUCUMBER

Plant seeds of this mild-tasting cucumber as you would those of any other cucumber. The vine will spread 4 or 5 feet in all directions and will need ample water and at least one feeding. The sooner you harvest the fruit, the better it will taste, but the cucumbers will grow as long as 2½ feet. Seeds for these slender, curving cucumbers are available in some nurseries and through mail-order catalogs.

Eggplant

Heat-loving relative to the tomato and pepper. Set out four plants to yield 12 eggplants in 2-3 months.

People who wrinkle their noses at the mention of eggplant are missing the gustatory delights of one of the best meat substitutes that can be grown in the garden. Prepared in cheese, egg, and tomato casseroles or sliced, batter-dipped and fried, eggplant can win over most doubters.

Eggplant fruits can be bitter when they pass the best harvest stage and seeds mature. Rarely, however, does a home garden produce bitter fruit, because gardeners tend to harvest eggplants before this point. Each plant should yield at least three to four fruits. Eggplants make excellent container specimens in tubs or boxes.

Eggplant is a heat-loving, frost-tender, summer vegetable. Because it sprouts and grows slowly from seeds, plants are customarily purchased. If eggplant is grown from seeds, a soil temperature of 75° is necessary for good sprouting.

Recommended varieties. The older, large-fruited market garden types, such as 'Black Beauty' and 'Burpee Hybrid', require 75 to 80 days to mature their first fruits. Over most of the country, the 65 to 70-day hybrids, such as 'Early Hybrid' and 'Morden Midget', will yield more fruit over a longer season, and the fruits will be of a more convenient size than those of the maincrop hybrids.

How to plant. Eggplant seeds sprout slowly; set out transplants after the ground warms up and all danger of frost is past. Space the plants 3 feet apart. If nights turn cold, protect the plants with a covering (see pages 38-39).

Care. Feed and water these as you do peppers. If you starve eggplant bushes or let them dry out, the fruit set will be sparse. Restrict the number of fruits on a plant to six by pinching off tip shoots and removing extra blossoms.

Pests. Colorado potato beetle can defoliate young plants. Control with rotenone, sevin, or diazinon. Eggplant lacebug, a troublesome pest in the South, feeds on the underside of leaves. Dust or spray with malathion. If aphids infest foliage, control them with rotenone or malathion (note label precautions). Wilt diseases of the same types that attack tomatoes and potatoes will sometimes affect eggplant. The only "cure" is to try to avoid it by rotating crops and not growing eggplant in places where tomatoes or potatoes have been grown in the past three years.

Harvesting. Pick when glossy, dark purple, and about 6 inches long. Use a knife or kitchen shears to snip off the fruits. Wear gloves—the stems are prickly. If some of the fruits reach full size and begin to lose their glossy sheen, don't eat them; cut off and discard the old fruit to encourage formation of new fruit.

In containers. Striking foliage, fruit, and blossoms and a worthwhile yield from a single plant make eggplant ideal for containers. Choose a tub or box with a capacity of at least 2 cubic feet.

Endive

Plant seeds of curly or broad-leafed type. Takes more heat than lettuce.

curly

French

If you are a salad lover, reserve a row in your late-summer garden for endive. A short row of 6 to 12 plants will give you a delicious substitute for lettuce until heavy frosts kill the plants. Endive plants are low growing and can spread to 18 inches wide.

Recommended varieties. 'Full Heart Batavian' is the smooth-leaved endive ordinarily sold as "Escarole." 'Green Curled' has deeply cut, curly leaves. Both mature in about three months from seeds; this dictates spring planting in cool, short-season areas.

How to plant. Endive is not particular about the type of soil you plant it in. Over most of the country, late summer plantings for a fall harvest are most successful. Plant seeds ¼ inch deep and 1 inch apart. In dry weather, dig a furrow 3 inches deep and scatter seeds in the bottom. Cover the seeds with 1 inch of soil and flood the furrow daily until the seeds sprout. Thin to 12 to 18 inches apart. Although hot-weather thinnings can be bitter in taste, the flavor will improve with cool weather and blanching.

Care. If the endive flavor is a little strong for your taste, gather the outer leaves up and tie them loosely. This will blanch the hearts and make them mild and tender. The best time to blanch is two to three weeks before the harvest stage.

Pests. Endive has few insect problems, but snails and slugs can eat the foliage. Spread ashes around the plants and pick the pests off at night. Or scatter snail and slug bait around the base of plants, watering to activate the bait.

Harvesting. A single head of endive can make salads for a small family, or outer leaves can be pulled off without harming the plant. Any excess endive can be cooked. You can protect late-maturing heads against freezing by mounding up soil or straw around them (see page 55).

In containers. The curly-leafed type is the most attractive. Sow a circle of seeds in a large tub or grow one plant per 8-inch pot.

FRENCH ENDIVE

You will also see this delicacy called Belgian endive, Witloof chicory, and *radicchio*. Because it takes special care, it's usually expensive.

Plant seeds indoors in flats, transplanting them in the spring into rich soil that has been worked to a depth of 18 inches. Keep the soil moist and weed-free. If growth is slow, apply a complete fertilizer.

In the fall, dig the mature plants carefully. Wash and trim roots to 9 inches long. Remove all the leaves except for the single central bud. The next step is forcing, which produces the pale cluster of well-blanched leaves. Place roots with buds pointing up in a 2-foot-deep bed of moist sand. Cover the roots with 6-10 inches of the sand kept damp and at room temperature. In 4 to 6 weeks, remove the blanched heads by pulling at the roots instead of tugging on the tender leaves. Cut the roots off before washing and serving the heads.

Herbs

Choose nursery plants of your favorites in early spring to add special flavor to your summer crops.

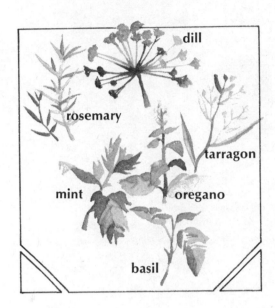

Tucked in the garden or growing in containers, fresh herbs provide fragrance and flavoring. Herbs include annuals, biennials, or perennials, but most of them thrive in full sun and in soil that is not too rich. (Too rich a soil dissipates their flavor.) Some of the most popular and useful herbs are listed here.

How to plant. Plant seeds of annual herbs in the ground or indoors in containers in the spring. If your soil tends toward acidity, add lime. Sow, thin, and cultivate as you would for vegetables. Nursery plants are practical if you only want a few.

Perennial herbs are usually sown in seed boxes and transplanted to flats or pots, from which they are planted into the garden. Many of them, such as rosemary and marjoram, are propagated from cuttings as well as from seeds. French tarragon does not produce seeds and can be grown from cuttings only.

Care. Herbs appreciate moderate amounts of complete fertilizer. Care for herbs in containers as described on page 7.

Harvesting and preserving. Herbs to be dried and stored should be harvested when the flavor-bearing oils are richest and most concentrated. With herbs grown for their leaves, this point is reached just as the flower buds begin to open or after the first flower has unfolded. Cut herbs early in the morning, but after any moisture on

Herbs dry *on racks made from dowels. They'll be ready to crumble and store in 3-7 days.*

BAY

This is actually a mild-climate tree (sweet bay or *Laurus nobilis*), the leaves of which are used for flavoring. Leaves of the California bay can be substituted.

Culture. Buy plants from a nursery, for seeds take a long time to germinate. This tree is frequently grown in large tubs on the patio. Many gardeners keep the head clipped in a rounded form.

DILL

Dill is an annual whose leaves and seeds are used fresh or dried in making pickles and in flavoring salads and many other foods.

Culture. Broadcast seed in spring after danger of frost is past. The spot should receive full sun and have good, well-drained soil. Thin the plants to 12 inches apart when they are 2 to 3 inches high. Or sow them in containers at least 10 inches deep.

Pinch off leaves to use any time after the plants are large enough to spare the foliage. Tie a small plastic bag over seed heads at maturity. When seeds begin to drop into the bag, brush remaining seeds into the bag and store.

MARJORAM

This tender plant is a perennial in mild-winter areas. Elsewhere, it's grown outdoors as an annual or indoors in containers. It is a bushy little plant about 2 feet high, with soft foliage and white flowers in knotted clusters. Use the leaves fresh or dried.

Culture. Marjoram likes full sun and fairly moist soil. Keep blossoms cut off and the plant trimmed to prevent woody growth. Propagate from seeds, cuttings, or root divisions.

MINT

There are many kinds of mint in popular use. The most common is the perennial spearmint, which grows to 2 feet tall and has dark green leaves with leafy spikes of purplish flowers. Use it fresh.

Culture. Mint takes full sun or partial shade. With adequate moisture, it spreads rapidly by underground stems. It is advisable to contain the roots in a box or pot to keep them from taking over the garden. Propagate mint from runners.

OREGANO

Also known as wild marjoram, this perennial grows to 2½ feet tall. Medium-sized leaves are oval shaped; blooms are purplish pink. Although oregano is best fresh, you can also use it dried.

them has dried. Strip the leaves from the stem, remove flower heads, and place the leaves loosely and thinly on trays with mesh bottoms through which air can freely circulate. The room in which the leaves are dried should be warm and dry, with no direct sunlight reaching the trays. Stir the leaves each morning for four or five days or until they are completely dry; then put them in airtight containers, such as glass jars. Or hang herbs in small bundles to dry.

BASIL

Sweet basil is a bushy annual that is easy to grow. The leaves and tender tips are spicy and flowerlike in flavor and odor. A few plants can be potted in the fall and brought indoors for winter use. Use basil fresh or dried. For contrast in an herb bed, look for the variety 'Dark Opal'. Its bronze foliage tastes similar to the green varieties.

Culture. Basil needs sun, average moisture, and light, well-drained soil. Plant seeds each month for a steady supply of the herb. Pinch out tips and flowers to keep plants bushy. Plants will produce two large crops a year.

Culture. Oregano likes sun, medium-rich soil, good drainage, and average watering. Keep the plant trimmed to prevent flowering. Replant every three years.

ROSEMARY

This half-hardy perennial has a sweet, fragrant scent, and the shrubs themselves are ornamental. Foliage is gray green; the flowers pale to dark blue depending on the variety. Shrubs reach 3 to 5 feet tall, but a spreading form is flatter.

Culture. Rosemary requires full sun and well-drained, gravelly soil that isn't too rich. The plant is drought resistant and can be propagated from cuttings.

SAGE

This is a shrubby perennial. The common form has gray green leaves with blue flowers. Other forms with the same flavor are 'Variegated Sage' with cream and purple leaf markings; and 'Golden Sage'. These varieties grow about 2 feet tall. 'Pineapple Sage' has mint green leaves with a pineapple flavor. It grows about 4½ feet tall and has vermilion flowers in late fall.

Culture. Sage likes sun and poor soil. It is fairly drought resistant. Cut the plant back after it blooms. Fertilize if you cut it continually. Divide the plants every three to four years. Propagate sage from cuttings or grow the common variety from seed (it germinates easily).

SAVORY

There are two kinds of savory—an annual summer type and a perennial winter type. Most popular is the summer savory, an 18-inch annual that grows easily from seed. The leaves of both kinds are narrow and green and are usable fresh or dried.

Culture. Savory likes full sun, an adequate amount of moisture, and light soil. Clip at the start of the flowering season for drying.

TARRAGON

There are two kinds: the marvelously fragrant and flavorful French tarragon, grown only from cuttings or divisions; and the unexciting Russian variety grown from seeds. The only way to be sure you are getting the French kind is to bruise a leaf to test for the strong fragrance. This kind grows into a perennial bush about 2 feet tall that dies back to the ground each winter.

Culture. This hardy plant thrives even in poor soil as long as it is well-drained. Give it some sun and normal watering. New plants can be started easily from divisions in the spring.

THYME

There are many kinds of thyme, all perennials and easy to grow. Some kinds grow 8 to 12 inches high; others form a mat close to the ground that you can walk on. Favorite kinds are 'Silver Thyme' with a cream border around the leaves; and 'Lemon Thyme' with a yellow border and lemony thyme fragrance and flavor.

Culture. Plant thyme in sun in light, sandy soil that is moderately dry (thyme thrives in hot, dry places where most other plants fail). Prune after flowering. Replant every three years. Thyme grows well from tip cuttings taken in spring and grows easily from seeds.

Horseradish

Grow in cool climates in rich, moist soil. Dig one root at a time to use when it's fresh and hot.

Horseradish root looks like an old dog bone. You can make horseradish sauce by peeling the root and blending it with vinegar. Grind together three parts horseradish cubes with one part white vinegar and a little salt. You can refrigerate the sauce for up to three months or freeze it.

How to plant. Buy a root at the store, stick it in the ground, and it should grow within a few weeks. It can be that easy. For more plants, buy a root with several crowns at the top end. Cut off each of these little crowns along with a wedge of the main root 2 to 3 inches long and plant them about 1 foot apart. Set the cuttings small end down and big end 2 inches below the soil surface. Plant them in a sunny place in loose, rock-free soil so the roots can grow uninhibited.

Harvesting. Roots grow most in late summer and early fall, so the best time to harvest is in October or November. From late fall through spring, dig up roots with a fork as you're ready to use them. Once your plants are fully established, you can probably dig some outer roots year round. Freshly dug roots are most flavorful.

In containers. The horseradish root is too large to be practical for containers.

Jerusalem artichoke

Plant tubers of this perennial in spring or fall. Foliage dies back in winter, regrows the following spring.

These tubers are a lazy gardener's dream plant—big crop for little effort. In food markets these tubers are relatively uncommon, but in a garden they grow and multiply like weeds.

You plunk the tubers into the ground as soon as soil is workable in spring (or in late fall). When the weather gets warm, up sprout spring plants that reach 6 feet or more. Yellow flowers bloom in late summer. Around November when leaves begin to die, you dig up big clumps of tubers to eat. They are crisp and sweet. Use them cooked or raw, somewhat like water chestnuts or new potatoes.

How to plant. Plant the tubers (or chunks with 2 or 3 eyes) 10 to 18 inches apart and 2 to 4 inches deep.

Care. Jerusalem artichokes aren't fussy about poor soil or scarce water (although they do best with reasonably rich soil and regular watering), but be sure to give them full sun. Choose firm, plump tubers from a grocery store or nursery (shriveled ones don't always grow); or order tubers by mail.

Harvesting. You may dig up plants with over 10 pounds of tubers each. This is delightful as long as you keep up with the harvest. If you want to prevent them from taking over your yard, it's wise to dig up excess tubers each spring. After being harvested in the fall, tubers dry out quickly, so store them in an airtight container in the refrigerator or in a cool place embedded in moist sand or sawdust. Better yet, dig only the amount you can use at one meal. They taste best immediately after harvest.

In containers. The plant's spreading habit makes it impractical for containers.

Kale

Stretch the season by planting kale for harvesting during cold weather since flavor is improved by light frosts.

Producing prodigious crops of sweet greens for cooking from summer through heavy frost, curly green kale is loaded with vitamins. The plants grow to 2 or 3 feet in height and equally as wide. If you keep such pets as guinea pigs, chickens, and rabbits, they will love fresh young kale leaves. And if you have always considered kale a "pot herb" for cooking, try tiny young leaves raw in salads. Plant kale in spring where summers are cool; plant after midsummer elsewhere. To harvest, cut off the outer leaves as needed. Pull smaller plants to thin.

For planting instructions and care see collards. Kale is subject to the same pests as cabbage; see that section for recommended controls.

Recommended variety. 'Dwarf Blue Curled'.

In containers. Use large containers and just harvest the outer leaves to keep plants growing all season.

Kohlrabi

Plant seeds of this cabbage relative in the spring garden for early summer harvest or the late summer garden for fall harvest.

A packet of kohlrabi seeds will give you buckets of delicious "above-ground turnips" for very little work. Spring-seeded kohlrabi sprouts and grows rapidly. When the plants are 6 to 8 inches high, the stems will begin to swell just above the root line until the "bulbs" are 3 to 4 inches across. Peeled and steamed, kohlrabi has a mild flavor somewhat like turnips—but far more delicate, with a crispness like that of water chestnuts. Try thin slices sauteed in butter.

Green and purple varieties are available; both have creamy white interiors. Kohlrabi matures in about two months. Eat kohlrabi when bulbs are 2 to 3 inches in diameter; they can get stringy when overly mature.

Broadcast seeds or plant them in wide bands. Thin to 12 inches apart. The young greens from thinnings can be combined with other kinds of greens and cooked. Kohlrabi can be stored much like turnips; see page 95.

In containers. Plants are unusual looking, grow rapidly, and will succeed in planters 8 to 10 inches deep.

Lettuce

Tuck seeds into any bare spot—different varieties in different spots for interesting salads.

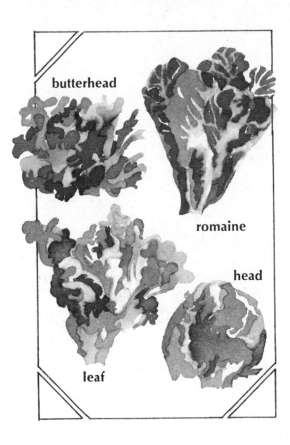

butterhead

romaine

head

leaf

Lettuce is one of the easiest of all vegetables to grow from seed. There are dozens of kinds and varieties to choose from. Dedicated lettuce fanciers can search seed racks and catalogs each planting season for new varieties to brighten the family salad bowl and surprise dinner guests. There are four types of lettuce. Leaf or loosehead lettuce forms a loose head that separates into large individual leaves for salads. It matures in 40 to 45 days. Butterhead forms small, rather open and irregular heads that blanch to a creamy interior color. It matures in 65 to 80 days. Romaine has upright, cylindrical, lightly folded heads that can easily be separated into individual leaves. It matures in 70 days if summer planted—80 if spring planted. Head lettuce requires 80 to 95 days to develop to full size.

Recommended varieties. Leaf lettuce varieties are 'Black Seeded Simpson', 'Salad Bowl', 'Oakleaf', 'Ruby' (reddish bronze), 'Grand Rapids', 'Prizehead', 'Green Ice' (slow to go to seed). Butterhead varieties are 'Bibb' (Limestone), 'Buttercrunch' (heat-resistant Bibb), 'Fordhook', 'Deer Tongue', 'Tom Thumb' (miniature). Romaine varieties are 'White Paris', 'Valmaine' (disease resistant). Good head lettuce varieties are 'Great Lakes,' 'Iceberg'.

How to plant. Lettuce is a cool-weather crop—there's no doubt about it. Lettuce not only sulks and goes to seed in hot weather, but the seeds will also refuse to sprout in very warm soil. Lettuce grows readily in cool soil, so make your plantings in very early spring and at two-week intervals until late spring. Then delay additional plantings until the weather cools off.

Quick-maturing leaf lettuce is the favorite where hot, humid summers follow closely on the heels of spring weather. In these areas, however, good fall crops of romaine or butterhead may be grown in fall if seeds are planted in late summer.

Spring crops of head lettuce from seeds sown indoors four to six weeks before the average frost-free date and set out as good-sized plants mature ahead of the warm weather. Fall crops of all types can be grown from seeds sown directly in the garden. In the northern tier of states, high-altitude gardens, and in cool coastal climates, lettuce can be grown all summer long.

Plant seeds ¼ inch deep and 1 inch apart in rows 18 inches apart. Set plants of heading varieties no less than 12 inches apart in rows 24 inches apart. If spaced more closely, they won't form large heads.

If you experience difficulty in sprouting lettuce seeds due to dry or hot soils, place a cupful of moistened sphagnum moss in a plastic bag and add a few dozen seeds. Store the bag in the vegetable freshener of the refrigerator during the day; take it out at night. The alternating temperatures should initiate sprouting within two to three weeks. Watch the seeds carefully and as soon as they show signs of sprouting, plant them— moss and all—during the cool evening hours. Cover with ¼ inch of soil and moisten the row thoroughly and often until the seedlings are established.

Care. Give leaf lettuce only a light fertilization at planting time; heading types will respond to a second light feeding when plants are half grown. Water lettuce lightly, but often.

Pests. Small green worms, slugs, and snails occasionally pester lettuce. Scatter bait on the ground to keep slugs and snails away. Pick off the green worms by hand.

Harvesting. Mature lettuce plants can be pulled for harvest, giving you a mixture of large and small leaves. If you have only a few plants, pull and eat just the outer leaves without sacrificing whole plants. Use all thinnings, of course, in salads. Leaf lettuce such as 'Grand Rapids' or 'Prizehead' can be cut off an inch or two above the ground and the plants will send out new leaves. Harvest head lettuce when the center feels firm.

In containers. Small size and fast growth make lettuce an ideal container crop. All you need is a soil depth of 6 inches and regular watering and feeding.

Melons

Summer plants with a voracious appetite for warmth, water, and space. The mouth-watering fruits take about 3 months to mature from seeds.

cantaloupe

watermelon

crenshaw

Like their fellow members of the cucurbit family (squash and cucumbers) melons thrive in warm weather, take up lots of space, and need regular, ample water. If you can provide these requirements, home-grown melons will reward you with a vine-ripened sweetness impossible to find in the market.

If you don't have a very long warm season, however, look for the earlier maturing hybrids that can be successful in all areas but those with the coolest or shortest summers. Compact varieties with short vines even make it possible to grow melons in a small garden.

The silvery green to buff or golden cantaloupe (muskmelon) are the fastest maturing and easiest to grow of the melons.

The long-season melons—such as the green-skinned 'Persian', the pink-fleshed 'Crenshaw', the lime green fleshed 'Honeydew', and the white-fleshed 'Casaba'— require up to 115 warm days to mature and dislike high humidity. They grow best in the warm interior valleys of the West and Southwest.

Watermelons—once considered long-season vegetables—can now be grown wherever cantaloupes mature reliably, thanks to new short-season varieties. The quick-maturing types called "icebox" melons have smaller fruits than those sold commercially. The large-fruited varieties require 85 to 90 days or more to ripen fully; they grow best in the Southern states and in warm Western interior valleys.

Recommended varieties. Cantaloupes: Early, compact varieties are 'Far North', 'Minnesota Midget'. Midseason spreading varieties are 'Burpee Hybrid', 'Samson Hybrid', 'Hale's Best', 'Iroquois'. Late melons are 'Persian', 'Casaba', 'Crenshaw', 'Honeydew'. 'Kazakh' is an early honeydew.

Watermelons: Early varieties are 'Golden Midget', 'Petite Sweet', 'Sugar Baby'. Midseason varieties are 'Sweet Princess', 'Fordhook Hybrid', 'Dixie Queen', 'Charleston Gray', 'Super Sweet', 'Crimson Sweet', 'Klondike', 'Peacock'.

How to plant. Unless you live where summers are long and warm both day and night, start melon seeds indoors in late spring in peat pots, large paper cups that can be torn without disturbing the root ball, or other deep, well-drained containers. Cover seeds with 1 inch of soil; they sprout at 75°. Seedlings will grow very rapidly in a sunny spot or under fluorescent lights, so don't start them more than two to three weeks before the frost-free date. Transplant carefully; melon seedlings have few

Stem pulls off *when cantaloupe is ripe. Clay pot support keeps fruit dry and insect-free.*

Midget watermelons *weigh less than standards, so you can train the vine up a trellis.*

Cantaloupe *trained to wire fence saves space. Larger fruits may need cloth sling for support.*

roots and are fragile. Set plants 3 to 8 feet apart, depending on variety.

Before planting seeds directly in the ground, wait until you find the soil has warmed to the 70-75° required to sprout seeds. Plant 1 inch deep in circles of 5 seeds and later thin to 3 plants per circle.

Melons respond dramatically to manure or fine compost in the soil and to being grown on mounds raised 6 inches above garden level for drainage and warmth. Build mounds for three plants by excavating about a bushel of soil, mixing with equal parts of organic matter and refilling the hole. Add a complete garden fertilizer when mixing the soil and feed plants every four to six weeks.

Grow melons in full sun at the side of the garden where the robust vines can be trained away from smaller vegetables. Vines are brittle and break easily, so train them while young. See page 8 for ideas on space-saving frames and supports.

Care. Mulch around the plants with straw to maintain an even level of soil temperature and moisture and to reduce loss of fruit to rotting. Watch the tips of vines for signs of wilting; then soak around the plants thoroughly.

Pests. Virus-carrying insects, such as cucumber beetles, can cripple young plants. If the plants slowly turn yellow and start to dry up, pull them up and replant. Spray with diazinon when beetles appear, stopping when label instructions indicate.

Harvesting. Here are some clues to ripeness in melons: for cantaloupes, if the stem slips off easily, the melon is ripe. Also, the opposite end softens and the netting becomes thick and corky as the fruit ripens.

For Persian and crenshaw, try the aroma test. Sniff the blossom end; if it smells sweet and fruity, the melon is ready. (Crenshaw can be fully ripe, yet have a green skin.) For honeydew and casaba, pick when the rind has turned deep yellow. The blossom end also tends to become springy instead of firm.

Even the experts are sometimes fooled by watermelons, but these tips can help you pick them at their prime. Rap the melon with your knuckles; a dull "plunk" means the watermelon is probably ready—a higher pitched "ping" means wait a few days and thump it again. (This test is most reliable in the early morning.) Also, note the two curly tendrils that extend from the stem nearest the fruit. When these turn brown, the melon is likely to be ripe. Check the light spot on the underside of the fruit. When this turns from white to light yellow, the melon is probably ready. Or, press down firmly on the top of the fruit with the palm of your hand. If you feel the flesh crack inside, it is ready to eat.

In containers. Large plants, slow growth, and low yield per plant make melons impractical for containers.

Mustard greens

Choose curly or smooth types. Plant seeds in the garden to mature during cool weather.

Plants of mustard grow knee high in 35 to 45 days and develop large, wide leaves. Cool weather improves the flavor. During hot weather the peppery tang to the greens can become strong, especially in older leaves.

Once flowering has started, it is useless to snap the tops off in the hope that new crops of leaves will form. Flowering is your signal to wait until cooler weather to plant a new batch of seeds.

Recommended varieties. Grow 'Florida Broad Leaf' where soils are sandy; the smooth leaves are easier to wash free of sand. 'Southern Giant Curled' is more handsome and has a fluffier texture in salads. 'Tendergreen' has broad, edible stems and matures rapidly; it is more tolerant of hot, dry weather.

How to plant. Mustard seeds sprout reliably in cool soil. The plants thrive in cool weather but quickly go to seed in the heat of summer. As early in the spring as the soil can be worked, plant seeds ½ inch deep and 1 to 2 inches apart. Thin plants to stand 2 to 3 feet apart. Eat the thinnings. Plant again in late summer. In mild winter areas, plant again in fall and winter.

Care. Fertilize lightly when seeds are planted. Water frequently and generously.

Pests. Hose off aphids and pick off cabbage worms or control them with *Bacillus thuringiensis* (note label precautions).

Harvesting. Pull plants only when thinning. Otherwise, snap off leaves, leaving the growing tip to produce replacements.

Leaves of 3 to 4 inches in length are tender enough to use in salads. Stringy stems are usually trimmed off larger leaves before the leaves are cooked.

Light frosts don't bother mustard; harvests can continue until heavy freezes wipe out the plants.

In containers. Fill boxes or pots with at least 6 inches of loose soil. Harvest outer leaves as you can use them.

Okra

If your garden will grow good sweet corn, it will grow good okra. Plant seeds when soil has warmed up.

Okra or Gumbo has a slightly mucilaginous consistency that takes some getting used to. However, when dipped in batter, breaded and fried, chopped for use in soup stock or sea food gumbos, or served with black-eyed peas, young okra pods are delicious.

Okra pods grow on large, erect, bushy plants with tropical-looking leaves. The pods appear where leaf stems join the main stem.

Recommended varieties. 'Clemson Spineless' has none of the prickles that make it necessary to wear gloves when harvesting other varieties. 'Dwarf Long Pod' has shorter plants than 'Perkins'.

How to plant. Okra seeds need a soil temperature of 70 to 75° to sprout. Sprouting can be improved by soaking seeds in water for 24 hours before planting. Sow seeds in groups of three in a sunny, well-drained area at the back of the garden where the large plants won't shade smaller vegetables. Mature plants should stand 3 feet apart.

Care. Okra plants are very heat resistant but need lots of water and fairly fertile soil (fertilize at least once during the growing season). Plants yield late and poorly where summers are cool. Elsewhere, late-spring planting will begin yielding in midsummer and continue until a killing frost. Eight to twelve plants should yield enough pods to feed four people.

Pests. Okra is troubled by few pests, but borers occasionally necessitate preventive sprays of sevin (note label precautions).

Harvesting. Pods should be harvested with a paring knife when they're 1 to 3 inches in length; they can get tough if allowed to go more than a day or two past their prime. Remove overripe pods to maintain vigor in plants.

In containers. The variety 'Red River' has a tropical look and in a large tub on a warm patio would yield enough okra to make one plant worth growing. Other varieties are too tall and rangy looking to be decorative.

Onion family

All members of the onion family dislike temperature extremes. Plant tiny onions called "sets" for a head start on the harvest date.

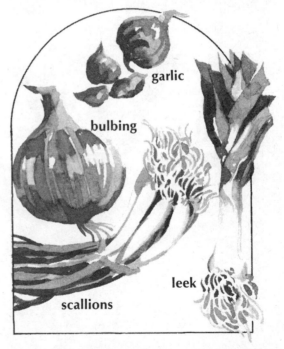

garlic

bulbing

leek

scallions

Onions may be easily grown from seeds, started plants, or "sets." If you want lots of green onions (scallions) or large, sweet, mild-flavored bulbs at low cost, start from seeds. In short-season areas, started plants of the mild Bermuda or sweet Spanish onions can bring in an earlier bulb harvest.

"Sets" are small bulbs of special varieties of onions. When you plant these tiny bulbs, the outer flesh sloughs off as new green scallions rise from the center of the bulb. Let them grow on from spring planting and they will form medium-sized, rather strong-flavored bulbs.

Recommended varieties. True bunching, non-bulbing types for scallions are 'Evergreen Bunching', 'Beltsville Bunching'. Spring-planted varieties for bulbs are 'Sweet Spanish', 'Autumn Spice', 'Southport Yellow Globe', 'Southport Red Globe', 'Fiesta Hybrid'. Fall-planted varieties for mild-winter areas are 'Bermuda' (yellow, red, and white), 'Granex', 'Grano', 'Italian Long Red' or 'Torpedo', 'Early Harvest No. 5 Hybrid'.

The varieties indicated for spring planting form bulbs only on shortening autumn days. Varieties for fall planting in mild climates form bulbs only during the lengthening days of spring.

How to plant. Onion family members like cool weather. Seeds sprout best in cool soil. Plant seeds ¼ inch deep and rather thickly; pull and transplant or eat the excess scallions. Plants should stand about 4 inches apart for bulb formation—1 to 2 inches apart for scallions.

Care. Onion family members have rather small root systems and need fairly frequent applications of fertilizer in order to form large bulbs. In heavy soil, grow them on raised beds for good drainage but keep the soil moist at all times to maintain steady growth. It is essential for good bulb formation to keep onions weeded, but roots are shallow and easily damaged by deep cultivation. Hand-pull weeds or just scrape the surface with a scuffle hoe.

Harvesting. Pull bunching onions or thin bulbing onions as soon as the scallions are big enough to make it worth the effort. Bulbing onions, garlic, and shallots must be completely dry to store well. When about half the tops have lopped over, break over the rest to hasten maturity. Dig up the bulbs and sun-dry them, making sure they are not bruised or soaked by rain showers and that the roots are completely out of the ground. (Roots covered with soil will continue to grow and the bulbs will become soft.)

In containers. The most popular members of the onion family for containers are green scallions and chives.

GARLIC

Plant the small bulb divisions or scales called "cloves" in the spring and in mild-winter areas also in October-December. Plant individual cloves with fat base downward 1 to 1½ inches deep and 2 to 3 inches apart in rows 12 inches apart. You'll have good-sized bulbs in 90 days. To store, hang and dry.

LEEKS

Grow these mild-flavored, mammoth, scallionlike plants from seeds planted in early spring. In hot

Peel *outer skin from leek in garden to keep dirt out of sink.*

Harvested leek *has bonus seedlings for next year's crop. Separate side shoots gently and plant into a new bed.*

Transplant leek seedlings *3 to 4 inches apart in furrows 5 inches deep. Cover with soil.*

climates, sow seeds in summer for winter harvests. Leeks can take as long as seven months to mature from seeds, and they dislike temperature extremes—these factors give them a reputation for being difficult in many areas.

In mild-winter areas, sow between August and mid-September. Elsewhere, sow as early as possible in spring.

Sow seeds directly in furrows or transplant from containers when about 4 inches tall. Transplant or thin to 3-4 inches apart. Space rows 6 to 12 inches apart. Plant in full sun near the coast or during cool weather; provide partial shade during hot weather.

As leeks grow, gradually mound loose soil around the stalks to blanch them, keeping the soil surface below the leaf joints so dirt doesn't work into the bulb end.

Harvest when leeks are from $1/2$ to 2 inches in diameter. Lift with a garden fork in heavy soil or root tips break off.

SHALLOTS

This small, onionlike plant produces a cluster of edible bulbs from a single bulb. The bulbs are prized in cooking for their distinct flavor.

Plant nursery plants, sets (small dry bulbs) from a seed store, or plant the bulbs you can buy in a grocery. Do the planting in fall in mild climates, early spring in cold-winter areas. Place in the ground so that the bulb tips are just covered.

At maturity, tops yellow and die. Harvest by pulling clumps and separating the bulbs. Let outer skin dry for about a month before using. You can store shallots for as long as six months.

Shallot varieties *grown in California (left) have thicker skins than larger, European varieties (right).*

Parsley

Good in containers or as edging for the garden. Supply fertilizers rich in nitrogen for lush green growth.

A plant or two of parsley should be enough to maintain a steady supply, because parsley plants quickly replace branches nipped off for the kitchen.

You can tuck parsley plants into sunny corners of flower beds or into rock gardens. The low, neatly mounded plants also make attractive edging or container plantings. Plants from the garden can be trimmed back severely in late summer, transplanted into pots, and grown on a window sill. You will have greater success with full sunlight.

Recommended varieties. 'Champion' or 'Moss Curled' is the favorite salad variety. 'Paramount' is darker green and more curled. 'Plain' or 'Single' holds its flavor in soups and stews. 'Hamburg' forms edible white roots.

How to plant. Parsley seeds take at least three weeks to sprout and then they grow so slowly that weeds tend to overgrow the seedlings. Buy plants or start seeds indoors (see page 29) and transplant them after danger of heavy frost is past. Sow seeds $1/4$ inch deep. Set in plants or thin to about 18 inches apart. Spring-planted parsley will produce until killed by heavy fall frosts. Parsley will live through the winter in mild areas and will shoot up seed stalks when the days grow long and warm.

Care. Give parsley a light feeding whenever its deep green color begins to fade. Water deeply.

Pests. Wildly-colored caterpillars often are attracted to parsley. Pick them off by hand. They give off a pungent odor as a defense mechanism.

Harvesting. For maximum flavor, pick parsley in the early morning hours before its delicate oils have evaporated. Pinch off older outer stems; leave the fresh new center growth to replace the pulled leaves. Small bunches can be hung to dry in the shade for making parsley flakes.

In containers. Ideal plant for a 8 or 9-inch pot. Frequent picking keeps new growth coming.

Parsnips

Long roots need loose, deeply worked soil. Long growing period takes patience.

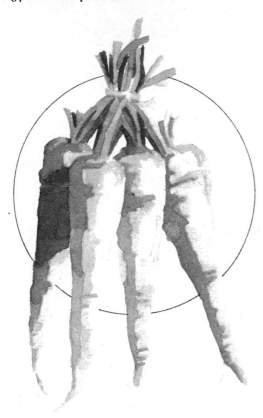

Culture of this root crop is much the same as for carrots and beets, but parsnips take much longer to mature from seed—about four months. Parsnip is a cool-weather crop; its roots are quite sweet after frost has intensified the sugar. In cold-winter areas, plant seeds in late spring, let them grow through summer, harvest them in fall, and leave the excess in the ground to be dug as needed all winter. In mild-climate areas, sow seeds in fall and harvest in spring. Soak parsnip seeds in water 24 hours before planting to improve germination.

Recommended varieties. 'Hollow Crown Improved', 'Harris Model', 'All American'.

How to plant. Prepare the soil deeply before planting, for some varieties are 15 inches long. Sow seeds ½ inch deep in rows 3 feet apart; thin to 6 inches apart.

Care. Follow the techniques for carrots and beets.

Pests. Parsnips are remarkably free from insects and diseases.

Harvesting. Pull parsnips before the tops begin to flower. Never leave parsnips in the ground past maturity, even in winter, for they will become tough and woody. Once picked, parsnips will keep for months in cool storage.

In containers. Roots are too large to make container growing practical.

Peanuts

Four months of warm weather and well-limed soil are basic to a successful peanut patch.

Yes, peanuts are vegetables and are not difficult to grow and prepare. Just ask any Southeastern resident who fixes boiled and salted peanuts or peanut soup. As vegetables or nuts, peanuts are interesting to watch and can reward you with a pint of peanuts per plant. Plants grow about 12 inches high and spread 2 to 3 feet across.

Peanuts mature in 110-120 days and show a decided preference for warm, well-drained, sandy or silty soil. One of the legumes, peanuts can use nitrogen from the air and don't need heavy fertilizing or rich soil. Following pollination, blossoms send little corkscrew tendrils into the soil. Almost every tendril will develop an underground cluster of well-filled peanuts.

Recommended varieties. The most common varieties are 'Jumbo Virginia', a large peanut with one or two big kernels in a pod and 'Spanish', with two or three smaller, sweeter kernels per pod. If you are in a short-season area, order seeds of 'Early Spanish'.

How to plant. Peanuts need lots of calcium. Dig in about 5 pounds of ground limestone per 100 square feet each spring (except on alkaline soil). Plant peanut seeds on built-up rows unless you have sandy soil. Shell the seeds without removing the thin red skins and sow them 1½ inches deep and 3 inches apart after all danger of frost is past and the soil is warm.

If you want only a few plants, start the seeds indoors in peat pots filled with sandy soil and transplant them before the roots start to penetrate the walls of the pots. Cover the young transplants until they get started.

Care. Peanuts require a light application of balanced fertilizer before planting and again in the middle of the growing season. They are not heavy drinkers. Don't cultivate around plant after pegs (just-forming peanuts) thrust themselves into the ground.

Pests. Especially in commercial growing areas, peanuts have their share of pests: caterpillars, cucumber beetles, leaf miners and thrips, to name a few. In other areas, peanuts can escape virtually unscathed. Use sevin in a preventive program for problem areas, following label directions carefully.

Harvesting. Harvest peanuts before fall frosts. Where summers are long, peanut plants will begin to turn yellow and die back when the nuts are ripe. Dig up the plants with a spading fork, carefully prying to keep from breaking up clusters. Gently knock off most of the soil. Place the plants in a warm, shaded, airy spot and allow the peanuts to dry. In two or three weeks, when the leaves are crumbly dry, pull the nuts off and store them in cloth bags. Allow them to dry thoroughly.

In containers. If soil is prepared as described above, peanuts will thrive in boxes or tubs with a soil depth of 12 to 18 inches.

Beginning of a peanut *or "peg" forms where each flower has faded in late summer.*

Peg buries itself *in soil, grows to proper depth; then peanut forms underground.*

Peas

The sweetest garden peas are produced during a long season of cool weather.

Only in areas that enjoy a fairly long period of cool weather do peas yield enough to justify the space occupied. Yet the taste of fresh garden or "English" peas is so mouth-watering that most gardeners will find the space for at least a short row.

(Continued on next page)

The length of row you plant depends on the variety and your climate. Where summers are quite cool or where mild winters with only light frosts provide three months or more of growing weather, the heavy-yielding, large-podded, tall or "pole" varieties may be grown. Elsewhere, the faster-maturing but lower-yielding "dwarf" varieties are more satisfactory. Their compact plants don't require staking or stringing. Three or four people can keep up with the output of a 10-foot row of tall peas or 20 feet of a dwarf variety.

Recommended varieties. Tall varieties are 'Alderman' and 'Melting Sugar' (edible-podded). Varieties 24 to 30 inches in height are 'Green Arrow', 'Little Marvel', 'Wando' (heat resistant), 'Morse's Progress No. 9', and 'Dwarf Gray Sugar'. The 30-inch, heavy-yielding 'Alaska' variety is often planted in the Southeast because its smooth seeds don't rot in cool soils as readily as the seeds of the wrinkle-seeded types.

How to plant. Where winters are mild, plant seeds in early fall so the plants will bear by midspring. Plant a second crop of a fast-maturing variety as early in the spring as the soil can be worked. Elsewhere, sow seeds as soon as the frost is out of the ground. Prepare the soil in the fall to permit earlier planting.

Sow seeds 1 inch deep in heavy soil, 2 inches in light soil, and 2 inches apart. If you are growing peas or beans in your garden for the first time, order a small packet of an "inoculant" from a seed catalog. This provides a special kind of soil bacteria that supplies peas with nitrogen for better growth.

Buy seeds already treated with fungicide when possible. In cool soil, at least half of the untreated pea seeds you plant will rot if a prolonged wet, cold spell arrives soon after planting. Raising the level of beds 6 inches above the surrounding soil will improve drainage and reduce rotting of seeds.

Care. For tall varieties, provide sturdy, 5-foot posts with wire stringers laced with twine. Tall peas do not twine but cling weakly and will need frequent tying up.

Peas, like beans, won't thrive in acid soil. (See page 21 for liming directions.) Go easy on adding compost and don't mulch peas; mulching keeps soil moisture at a high level and the soil cooler than is best for peas. Work in a light application of low-nitrogen fertilizer when preparing beds; reapply 30 days later by watering-in fertilizer.

Water peas with a soaker or through irrigation furrows. Overhead watering encourages mildew.

Toward the season's end, plants tend to mildew despite careful watering. You can retard it by dusting with sulfur.

Pests. Control pea aphids and weevils with diazinon (note label precautions).

Harvesting. Begin harvesting when pods have swelled to almost a round shape and pick them every few days. Don't let any overly mature pods remain on the plants;

they reduce the total yield. Always grasp the pea vines with your free hand when pulling peas to prevent damage to the brittle vines. Pick sugar peas (edible-podded or Chinese) when pods are 2 to 3 inches long and while the seeds are still undeveloped.

In containers. Deep roots, a need for even moisture, and the number of plants required make peas an impractical container choice.

Peppers

Pick your snappiness quotient from mildly pungent to eye-watering. Set out plants in warm weather.

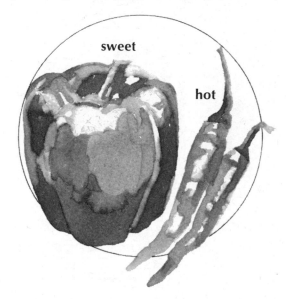

sweet

hot

Dozens of varieties are available within the two major types of peppers: sweet (or bell) and hot. If a pepper is even mildly pungent, it is classed as hot. Fruits of most pepper varieties are green when young and red at maturity but are delicious at all stages. Some varieties are yellowish green to bright yellow when ripe.

Sweet peppers grow on stiff, rather compact, large-leafed bushes about 16 inches high. True hot pepper plants are taller, more spreading, and have smaller, narrower leaves. Sweet peppers mature in 65 to 80 days and can be grown anywhere in the country except in high elevations or extreme northern areas. Hot peppers ripen later and are better suited to areas with long, warm seasons, but they can be grown in northern states.

Recommended varieties. Sweet varieties resistant to tobacco mosaic are 'Peter Piper' hybrid (early), 'Bell Boy' hybrid, 'Yolo Wonder'. Other sweet varieties are 'Keystone Giant', 'Vinette' (miniature), 'Pimento', 'Canape' hybrid, 'California Wonder', 'Golden Calwonder', 'Sweet Banana'. Hot varieties are 'Cayenne', 'Red Chili', 'Tabasco', 'Chili Jalapeno' (very hot), 'Hungarian Yellow Wax', 'Anaheim', 'Rumanian Hot'.

How to plant. Peppers are slow to start from seeds; about eight weeks are required to grow your own to transplant stage. If you start from seeds, plant them ⅛ inch deep and sprout at a steady temperature of 70 to 80° day and night. Transplant in early summer after frost danger has passed. Set plants 2 feet apart and no deeper than they grew in the flat.

Care. Peppers should be fed every 30 to 45 days with a complete fertilizer. Too much nitrogen can cause rank growth and a poor set of blossoms. For maximum continued yields, water once or twice weekly; dry soil can inhibit fruit formation.

Pests. Few bugs bother peppers, but aphids can transmit viruses from plant to plant. If any plants become stunted or mottled from the "mosaic" virus, pull the plants out before the virus spreads. There is no practical way to save infected plants.

Harvesting. Clip off peppers as soon as they are of a usable size or when they turn to their mature color. Leaving overripe peppers on the vines can reduce yields by draining food reserves. When growing hot peppers for dry storage, let them turn red before picking. Don't rub your eyes if you have been picking hot peppers; the juice is irritating. You might wear gloves if you have quite a few to pick.

In containers. Compact plants, decorative fruits, and sustained, heavy yield make peppers ideal for containers. Provide ¾ to 1 cubic foot of soil per plant.

Potatoes

Plant sets in early spring—be prepared for space demand and requirement for well-drained soil.

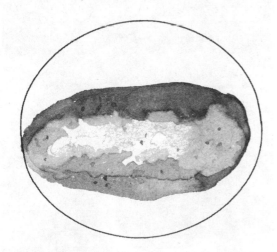

You need a good-sized, sunny plot to grow potatoes. Vines grow about 2 feet high and are very leafy; the potato tubers form underground.

Potato vines rarely form seeds; garden potatoes are grown from "sets," which are chunky segments cut from certified, disease-free tubers. Sprouts grow from the eyes, so each set should have at least two eyes. Upper portions of the sprout become tops; lower portions form roots and short stems. Sets are hard to find in most localities but can be ordered from one of the mail-order seed companies. Potatoes from produce racks are often treated with a sprout inhibitor and won't grow properly if cut up for sets.

Recommended varieties. 'Kennebec' and 'Bake King' (white); 'Norland' (early red).

How to plant. Very early spring planting is required except where winters are mild. In such areas crops can be planted in July for a late fall harvest.

Potatoes need a sandy, fast-draining soil; tubers become deformed in heavy, poorly drained soil. If your soil is heavy, use the following method for planting. (In any case, do not plant if soil is very wet.) Remove 2 to 3 inches of soil from the row, setting it aside. Spade deeply and fertilize. Soak the soil deeply; then let it dry for two to three days. Make a 3-inch layer of compost or spoiled hay down the length of the row. Lay the eyes 12 to 18 inches apart, the cut side down on the organic matter. Cover with another 3 inches of garden soil to keep the rough material from blowing. Large, clean tubers will form on underground stems within the warm, decomposing layer, simplifying harvesting.

Care. Because the layer of organic matter will interfere with capillary moisture flow from below, you will need to lay a soaker upside down on the row and water thoroughly every two to three weeks in dry weather. If you grow potatoes without the organic matter, apply water through irrigation furrows to avoid wetting the foliage. Knobby potatoes result if the soil dries out (stopping growth) and is wetted again.

Pests. Name almost any beetle, borer, leafhopper or caterpillar—potato vines will attract them, along with blights, leaf fungi, and tuber scab. Consult your farm advisor on the best preventive materials for your area and for the timing of controls.

Harvesting. Dig up early varieties when flowers form on the plants; on later varieties, yellowing and dying of vines will indicate the tubers have reached full size. Loosen the soil with a spading fork along the outer edges of the bed. Probe carefully so you don't impale tubers. Then, slide the spading fork under the central plant, lifting and shaking gently to remove tubers. Turn the loose soil over to find the small tubers that escaped the lifting. Don't bruise tubers or let them stand in the sun. Store them in a cool, dark area, unwashed, until ready for use. Well-matured potatoes free of defects store best.

In containers. Wide-spreading root system makes the potato a poor candidate for container growing.

SWEET POTATOES

This plant of tropical origin likes long, hot summers. Sweet potatoes also demand lots of space and well-drained soil, preferably sandy loam.

Start sweet potatoes from nursery plants or from slips. To get slips, plant the whole tuber of the variety you like in water or in sand. Use toothpicks to suspend them in water if you are just planting a few. Otherwise, plant the tubers in a deep bed of sand kept at a temperature of 70 to 75° in a hotbed or coldframe. When sprouts reach 9 inches, cut them off and plant these slips in sandy soil. Allow at least one foot between plants. Vines will spread 6 feet or more across.

Water frequently but don't feed with too much nitrogen or you will find all vine and no potatoes. Normal vine growth is usually lush enough to overpower weeds. Cover newly-planted slips if the temperature dips.

In the fall before frost arrives, dig the tubers, being careful not to bruise the roots. If you are going to store the potatoes, don't wash them. Dry them at 80 to 85° for two or three weeks before storing them for the winter.

Gopher *bur-rowed beneath pumpkin on the ground and ate the whole thing.*

Board under pumpkin *keeps gophers out, also prevents fruit from rotting on moist ground.*

Pumpkins

Choose small varieties for pie or big ones for the thrill of watching them grow into jack-o-lantern candidates. Plant seeds in the garden when the weather has warmed.

Pumpkin vine *climbs fence to save space; cloth sling gives heavy fruit extra support.*

You can grow pumpkins for cooking, canning, edible seeds, Halloween pie decorations, or just for the fun of it.

Varieties range in size from tiny jack-o-lanterns to giants weighing more than 100 pounds.

Planting a pumpkin vine in a small garden is analogous to letting a camel put his nose in your tent. The first thing you know, the rampant running vines will have taken over. Even the newer "bush" types spread over 20 square feet in rich soil.

Recommended varieties. Bush type (95-day maturity, 7-lb. fruits): 'Cinderella'. Halloween type (110 days, 10 to 20-lb. fruits): 'Jack O'Lantern'. Mammoth type (120 days—fruits up to 100 lbs. or more): 'Big Max' (pinkish-orange) and 'Hungarian' (gray). 'Lady Godiva' is grown for its hull-less edible seeds; you just roast and eat them.

How to plant. Start pumpkins from seeds sown in the garden in early summer. Little is to be gained by starting seeds indoors because transplanting sets them back. Plant seeds in circles of three, raised slightly for drainage and warmth.

Care. Feed plants twice with a balanced fertilizer before the vines spread too thickly for the fertilizer to reach the roots.

There are many theories on how to grow mammoth pumpkins. One effective way is to plant the seeds (or seedlings started in peat pots) on top of a heap of well-rotted compost. Water the vines when you see the slightest sign of wilting and feed heavily every 10 to 14 days with a dilute solution of plant food or manure water. Pinch off all but one or two pumpkins per vine. While the pumpkins are still small, lay them on wide squares of plywood to keep snails or slugs from burrowing into the fruit.

Another good way to grow big pumpkins is to scoop a hole 4 inches deep the length of the seedbed and fill with a shovelful of manure. Cover with enough soil to bring the bed up to ground level and plant the seeds in this soil. Water, feed, and pinch off as described above.

Pests. Vine borers can be a major pest but are hard to kill with sprays. Look for holes with yellowish material coming out and slit the stalks at those places with a razor blade to remove the borers. Then heap a shovel of soil over the injured area. If the vines are vigorous, they will set roots at that point and outgrow the damage. Late-season mildew is almost unavoidable. The best preventive is to plant pumpkins where they get plenty of air movement and no overhead sprinkling.

Harvesting. Be careful not to handle green pumpkins more than necessary, for they bruise easily. When the pumpkin is ready, the skin color darkens, the skin becomes tough, and the vines dry up. Cut off pumpkins before a heavy frost comes, leaving 3 to 4 inches of stem on the fruit. If just a light frost is expected, a straw covering piled on top of the fruit is usually sufficient protection. Don't wash the fruits before storing. Store them in a warm, dry place.

In containers. Huge plants disqualify pumpkins from growing in all but the most giant containers.

Radishes

Sow seeds here and there—harvest radishes in as little as 3 weeks. Avoid hot weather harvests.

Easy and fast to grow, radishes are not usually planted in special rows. Sow a pinch of radish seeds at a time here and there among slow-sprouting seeds of other vegetables or in unused corners. You might try mixing radish seeds with carrot, parsnip, or parsley if your soil is likely to form a crust. The vigorous radish seedlings will break through and open the way for the weaker seeds that might not otherwise make it. Within three and a half to four weeks of planting, the radishes will have matured and can be pulled. A packet of seeds will usually yield several dozen radishes.

Recommended varieties. Radish varieties differ in color, shape, mildness of flavor, and speed of maturity. Early, fast-growing varieties for spring sowing are 'Cherry Belle', 'French Breakfast', 'Sparkler', 'Icicle' (looks just like its name). 'Crimson Giant' grows large without becoming pithy. These summer radishes are slow growing but stand up better to hot weather: 'All Seasons White', 'White Strassburg'. These large, late-maturing "winter radishes" can be planted in late summer in mild climates for winter harvests: 'Long Black Spanish', 'Sakurajima', 'White Chinese', or 'Celestial'.

How to plant. Radishes are frost hardy. Sow seeds as soon as the soil can be worked in the spring and at two week intervals thereafter except during the hottest part of summer. Summer-grown roots turn pithy rapidly, or plants shoot to seed. Work in a light application of balanced fertilizer, plant seeds ½ inch deep and 1 inch apart, and water weekly.

Pests. If you have had problems with grubs (maggots) boring into the roots, apply diazinon right in the furrow when you sow the seed, following label directions carefully. Any spraying after that should be done before the roots have started to swell. Summer-grown radishes are the most susceptible. Leaf miners can disfigure the leaves, but this has little effect on the roots.

Harvesting. Begin pulling radishes when they are a little larger than a pea. Pull out and discard plants as soon as roots begin to get pithy or pungent.

In containers. A soil depth of only 4 to 8 inches is needed for this fast-growing crop.

Rhubarb

Start harvesting a year after planting roots or transplants. Bushy plant is productive for at least 8 years. Partial shade or sun.

The beauty of this perennial has been its salvation in the home garden because, in most areas, its harvest season is rather short to justify the care and space it needs for an entire season. The broad, pink-tinged, crumpled leaves on tall, smooth stalks make interesting focal points in flower beds or in tubs. Six to eight plants

Bottomless basket *protects rhubarb, keeps stalks off ground, marks root location in winter.*

of this massive, hardy perennial will keep you in rhubarb pies throughout the spring.

Rhubarb dies back or goes dormant each fall and shoots up new leaves in the spring. The plant needs a dormant period and doesn't do well in the Southeast, along the Gulf Coast, and in parts of the Southwest where winters are warm. In mild-winter areas summer dormancy can be achieved by cutting back on water for several weeks after the plant has stopped producing stalks.

Recommended varieties. 'Victoria' is available in seeds. Better varieties, such as 'MacDonald', 'Valentine', 'Cherry', 'Strawberry', are available in roots or plants.

How to plant. Sow seeds or set out young potted plants or roots in late spring. Space plants 4 to 6 feet apart. The first heavy harvest can be taken the third spring.

Care. Feed rhubarb plants in the early spring and again in early fall. In areas where the soil freezes deeply, mulch rhubarb in winter after the soil has frozen. Apply 3 to 4 inches of compost or manure (not leaves) to prevent the soil from heaving and to add humus. Rhubarb is deep-rooted; water plants every two to three weeks by soaking the soil deeply around the crowns.

Pests. Rhubarb has few pests.

Harvesting. Give clumps a year to become established before harvesting (rhubarb sown from seeds needs two years). Using a sideways twist, snap off stems at the base when they reach 12 to 18 inches in length. Trim off and discard all of the leaf blades; they are mildly poisonous. Leave a few stalks on each plant to manufacture food and rebuild the energy in the crown.

In containers. Rhubarb makes a handsome container plant in a minimum of 3 cubic feet of soil per plant. If frost hits, move the container into a cool garage or cellar.

Salsify

Sow seeds in early spring. Wait up to 5 months to harvest the long, whitish roots.

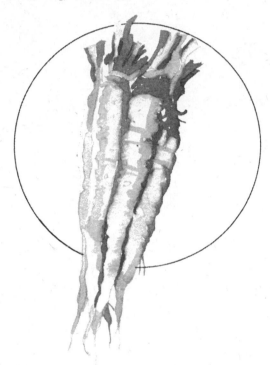

The distinctive flavor of the salsify root has earned it the name "oyster plant." It looks much like a parsnip, however, and takes a long time to mature from seed like a parsnip—up to 150 days. A bed 8 feet by 3 feet will support about 30 large roots from two rows.

Recommended variety. 'Sandwich Island Mammoth' is the popular favorite.

How to plant. Since salsify is a long-season crop, it should be intercropped with something fast, such as lettuce, spinach, radishes, or Swiss chard. Work the soil to a depth of at least 18 inches so that it will be loose and crumbly. Sow the seed in rows 15 inches apart, covering them with ½ inch of fine soil. When plants are about 2 inches high, thin them out to 3 inches apart.

Care. Follow instructions for carrots and beets.

Pests. Salsify is seldom bothered by pests or diseases.

Harvesting. Don't pull the roots out of the ground too forcibly, or you will break them.

In containers. Roots are too large to make container growing practical.

Spinach

This leafy crop just can't take long days and hot temperatures. Plant seeds right after frost for spring harvest or in late summer for fall harvest.

Fast-growing, short-lived spinach will mature its leafy plants in seven weeks; then it quickly goes to seed. Plant short rows every two to three weeks to maintain a supply. Spinach definitely prefers cool weather and needs to be grown rapidly to form large, meaty leaves.

Recommended varieties. 'America', 'Bloomsdale Long Standing', 'Nobel'. New Zealand spinach, which forms short runners, resembles regular spinach in leaf shape but tolerates warm weather much better. It is not a true spinach but will be productive all season and is delicious raw in salads or cooked.

How to plant. Plant spinach seeds very early in the spring and periodically through early fall except during the hottest days. Plant New Zealand spinach in late spring. Sow seeds ½ inch deep. Thin to 8 inches apart; use the thinnings for salads.

Care. Nitrate forms of nitrogen fertilizer release more readily in cool weather and will help to produce good early spring, late fall, or winter crops of spinach.

Pests. Leaf miners and aphids frequently attack spinach. Hose aphids off or try washing the leaves with a soap and water solution (see page 54).

Harvesting. Nip off the outer leaves; discard the stems if they are stringy. Leave the center sprouts to form new leaves. When you first see flower buds forming in the center of the plant, quickly harvest the entire crop and use it rather than letting the spinach set seeds and be wasted.

In containers. A good crop for boxes or pots. New Zealand spinach is particularly suited to containers because it grows back quickly after cutting. Grow one plant of the New Zealand variety per 2-gallon container. Soil depth should be about 8 to 12 inches.

Squash

Once the weather warms, expect prolific growth and high yields of summer squash, large fruits on winter squash.

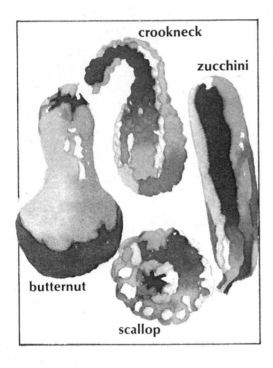

crookneck

zucchini

butternut

scallop

Names scratched *in young winter squash with nail or knife tip grow with the vegetable.*

You will find two types of squash. Summer squash, the faster growing, smaller fruited type, is planted for warm-weather harvest and eaten when young — skins, immature seeds, and all. Winter squash is planted and grown just like the pumpkin, which it resembles in vine size and fruiting characteristics. Summer squash can yield prodigious crops from just a few plants and will continue bearing for several weeks. The bushes are large — 2½ feet x 4 feet across at maturity — and will overgrow smaller vegetables unless given plenty of room. Winter squash, a rampant grower with bigger fruits, is grown for late harvest and winter storage. The skin is hard and inedible. Scoop out seeds and pulp before baking. Seeds may be saved, dried, and roasted.

Recommended summer varieties. Green zucchini types are 'Aristocrat', 'Burpee Hybrid', 'Cocozelle'. Packets are sometimes labeled simply "Black" or "Green" (zucchini). Yellow types are 'Early Prolific Straightneck', 'Yellow Summer Crookneck'. Patty pan or scallop types are 'St. Pat Hybrid', 'White Bush Scallop'. 'Golden Zucchini' is a yellow zucchini.

Recommended winter varieties. Bush types are 'Kindred', 'Bush Ebony', 'Bush Table Queen'. Vining or running types are 'Butternut', 'Golden Nugget', 'Hubbard', 'Banana', 'Waltham', 'Green Cushaw'.

How to plant. Wait until frost danger is past and the soil is warm. Plant seeds 1 inch deep in circles of three to five, spaced 4 to 5 feet apart. Later thin to two plants per circle (see page 34).

Care. Since squash loses lots of water through its large leaves, water heavily and frequently. Mulches help conserve moisture and decrease loss of fruit to rotting. (See page 47.)

Squash needs plenty of fertilizer to replace the nutrients removed by heavy growth and prolific fruit production. Dry fertilizers are hard to apply because of the heavy foliage canopy. Feeding and watering can be accomplished at the same time by planting seeds around a 2 to 3-gallon can that has been perforated and sunk into the ground. Fill it full of water twice weekly and with a dilute solution of fertilizer at least once a month.

Pests. Squash vine borer can be serious, particularly east of the Rockies. (For control, see page 89.) Squash bugs are difficult to control. The best method is to hand pick and destroy both the bugs and the leaves that contain the eggs. Also, remove all debris that would give winter shelter. Mildew is usually heavy in late fall; to reduce it, avoid overhead watering.

Harvesting. Pick yellow varieties when pale yellow rather than golden. Harvest scalloped squash when small and greenish, before they turn white.

Summer squash should be picked before the skin turns hard; test it with your thumbnail for tenderness. From 4 to 8 inches long is the best harvest stage; the seeds and skin begin to get hard and tough in larger fruits. To prolong the harvest period, pick frequently and do not allow any fruit to reach large size.

Harvest winter squash in late fall after the vines have dried but before a heavy frost. The skin of fruits should be hard when tested with your thumbnail. Stems are thick; cut them with a sharp knife, leaving a 2-inch stub. Store the squash in a warm, dry place.

In containers. Squash plants are too big for all but the largest containers.

SPAGHETTI SQUASH

This squash looks like any other winter squash, but the flesh is made up of long, spaghetti-sized strands. You can bake the whole squash and then serve the insides with just butter or any sauce that goes on spaghetti.

Plant seeds or started plants in spring in a sunny spot. Plants should be 5 to 8 feet apart. Vines will start bearing fruit in about 90 days. A handful of fertilizer in the soil will get them off to a good start.

A squash is ready to pick when the skins turn golden yellow; they will grow to between 4 and 6 pounds.

Baked spaghetti squash *reveals strands that taste more like squash than spaghetti, grow just like any squash.*

Tomatoes

Harvest juicy tomatoes in as little as two months of warm weather after setting out plants.

King of the vegetable garden, the tomato outranks all others in popularity. Tomatoes reward gardeners handsomely for their small investment of time and space.

Recommended varieties. Varieties differ in size of plant; in size, shape, color, and taste of fruit; and in their adaptability to different climates. Plants sold at nurseries are usually the best ones for the local climate.

Tomatoes with small fruits come on both large and small vines. 'Tiny Tim' and 'Pixie' bear small red fruits on vines about 18 inches high. 'Patio' bears ping-pong ball-sized fruits on slightly larger vines. 'Red Cherry' grows small red fruits on large vines. 'Yellow Pear' produces small pear-shaped tomatoes on large vines.

Early-fruiting tomatoes need less heat to ripen fruit than other varieties. In climates where spring and summer nights are warm, plant them to get ripe tomatoes as early as six weeks to two months after setting out plants. In climates where spring and summer nights are cool or cold, plant this kind to get tomatoes at all. 'Tiny Tim', mentioned above, is very early (45 to 55 days). 'Earliana' needs only 60 days, and 'Spring Giant' needs 65 to 70. 'Early Girl' ripens in 55 to 60 days.

Hybrid tomatoes grow more vigorously and produce larger and more uniform fruit than other varieties. There are many in this group; two favorites are 'Better Boy' and Burpee's 'Big Boy'.

Large, red, standard tomatoes produce broad, meaty, tasty fruit on large vines about three months after planting. 'Ace' and 'Beefsteak' are two good ones; the latter is sometimes called pink rather than red.

(Continued on next page)

Pruning *some of the side shoots on tomato plant redirects energy from new growth to fruiting.*

Plastic film *secured over roots of young tomato plant warms soil to speed root growth.*

Some tomato varieties were developed to grow and bear in soil that is infested with organisms that can otherwise be fatal to tomato plants—verticillium wilt, fusarium wilt, and nematodes. The variety names and seed packages either say so or they carry the letters V, F, or N after the variety name to indicate resistance to any or all of these troubles.

How to plant. The choice of tomato varieties in stores is often limited. Send away early for seeds, and start them indoors six weeks before frost danger is past. Harden off tomato plants, including purchased plants, before setting them into the garden. Tomatoes cannot withstand frost; wait until late spring to transplant into the garden.

Set plants out when they are 6 to 10 inches tall, 24 to 48 inches apart. Work a complete fertilizer into the planting bed according to label directions. Set the plants in deeply—you can bury as much as half to three quarters of the leafless part of the stem (see photo on page 40). Roots will form along the buried part of the stem and make the plants grow stronger.

To save space and make tomato growing easier, install stakes before you plant. Unstaked vines will sprawl across many square feet and some fruits will lie on the soil, often causing rot, pest damage, and discoloration. A 6-foot-long stake (at least 1-by-1 inch) driven into the ground at least a foot from each seedling is the simplest method to install. A cylinder of welded wire is more trouble to install but makes it easier to train vines. Put stakes at opposite sides of each cylinder and tie it firmly to them. Poke vine branches into openings in the cylinder as the plant grows. (Other staking ideas on page 8.)

Care. Cut off the suckers that form between the branches and main stem to open up vines and to encourage opening of fruit.

Irrigate tomato plants frequently during the early part of the season, less frequently after fruit begins to set.

Tomatoes will pollinate reliably at 65° for late varieties, at 60° for early varieties. Fruit-setting hormones are worth the expense where summer nights are cooler.

Dig in a bushel of compost or rotted manure for each plant, mulch with straw or plastic, and feed with a complete fertilizer. Some of the heaviest yields recorded have been made with the full-season, controlled-release fertilizers.

Tomatoes should be watered deeply at least every 10 days during dry spells. Blossom drop can be caused by too much or too little water.

Pests. Tomato hornworms, though bizarre and menacing looking, won't harm you and can be picked off by hand. Whiteflies can gather in great numbers underneath leaves without doing much damage. Blights, viruses, and wilts are usually the reasons for mysterious shriveling and death. Look for streaks, blotches, curly tops (some curling is normal). Pull out sick plants and try disease-resistant varieties next time.

Harvesting. For fresh use, harvest at the stage of ripeness that most appeals to you. For juice or canning, fruit can remain on the vine for several days past the best harvest stage while you are waiting for enough fruits to ripen to make preserving worthwhile. Large green tomatoes will ripen in several weeks in a cool, humid dark place (around 60°).

In containers. Although any tomato plant can grow in a large enough container, the midget varieties are best suited for pots with a soil capacity of 1 cubic foot (see recommended varieties above). Provide tubs with a soil capacity of 3 cubic feet for the standard sized plants. Set stakes in the soil at the time of planting and tie foliage to them as it grows. Small-fruited cherry and pear tomatoes are ideal for hanging baskets (see page 36). Tomatoes are also well suited to hydroponic culture (see page 50).

Turnips and Rutabagas

Plant turnip seeds to harvest in spring or fall, rutabaga seeds for fall and winter harvest.

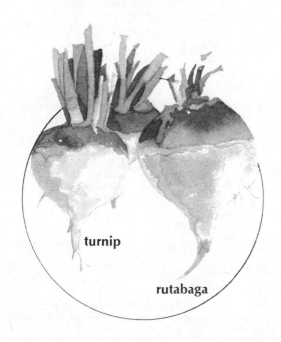

turnip

rutabaga

These cool-season, frost-hardy cousins produce huge crops of edible roots and greens from a given area. Both

spring and fall crops of turnips are possible, but rutabagas are almost always planted in midsummer for a late fall harvest. Turnips require 45 to 60 days to mature roots; rutabagas, 90 days. The heavy tops of rutabagas are edible but coarse. Turnip greens are very popular, cooked alone or mixed with diced or sliced turnip roots or in equal parts with mustard greens. Special, very hardy varieties with nonedible roots are favored for a fall and winter harvest of greens in the Southern states.

Turnip plants can reach about 18 inches in height and spread but can be spaced closely for intensive gardening. Rutabaga plants are much larger and are generally widely spaced to allow the large roots to reach their full weight of 3 to 5 pounds each. Rutabaga roots can be kept in cool storage if washed, trimmed, dried thoroughly, and dipped in wax.

Different varieties give a nice choice of colors and shapes. Turnips can be globe shaped or a flattened globe. Colors are white, white topped with purple, or creamy yellow. Rutabagas have large, yellowish roots, sometimes topped with purple.

Recommended varieties. Turnips for roots and greens: 'Golden Ball', 'Purple Top White Globe', 'Just Right', 'Tokyo Cross'. For greens only: 'Seven Top', 'Shogoin'. Rutabagas: 'American Purple Top', 'Laurentian', 'Altasweet'.

How to plant. Work plant food into the bed and broadcast a second application around plants a month later. For spring crops, plant seeds ¼ inch deep in short rows as early in the spring as the soil can be worked. For fall harvest, sow seeds ½ inch deep in midsummer. Broadcast turnip seeds or sow them thinly in rows 18 inches apart. Sow rutabaga seeds 1 to 2 inches apart in rows 30 inches apart.

Care. During dry weather, two or three waterings per week will be needed to prevent wilting of foliage.

Pests. Control root maggots on summer-planted crops with diazinon in the furrow before planting seeds. If they persist, don't plant during warm weather. Control aphids and cabbage loopers with malathion. Follow label directions when applying chemicals.

Harvesting. Pick greens while they are the size of your hand or smaller; the stems of older leaves get stringy. Begin pulling turnip roots when they reach 2 inches in diameter. Roots will keep in the ground until the soil begins to freeze solid. Then they can be dug and topped and stored in a straw or leaf pile or a very cool root cellar. Pull and top rutabagas before roots are injured by extreme cold.

In containers. Both these root crops require a great deal of soil depth to be successful. Try kohlrabi instead—it's prettier, grows faster, and produces its crop above ground.

Index

Photographers

William Aplin: 12; 13 top; 25 left; 40 left; 44; 59 left; 67; 74; 78; 79 left; 80; 82 top right; 94 left. **Dave Cavender:** 48 bottom left. **Glenn Christiansen:** 34 top; 54 bottom right; 93. **Patricia Clifford:** 9 center, right. **Gerald R. Frederick:** 20 left; 45 right. **Steve Lorton:** 7 right; 92. **Bill Marken:** 5 bottom left; 94 right. **Ells Marugg:** 5 bottom right; 13 bottom; 17 bottom. **John McClements:** 48 right. **Don Normark:** 17 top; 20 bottom; 22; 23; 36 left; 52; 59 right; 66; 71 right; 90. **Steve Peithman:** 9 left. **Norman A. Plate:** 4; 5 top left; 26; 34 bottom; 40 right; 45 left; 69; 79 right; 88 bottom. **Pete Redpath:** 14. **Darrow M. Watt:** 5 top right; 7 left; 18; 20 top right; 24 right, left; 25 top right, bottom; 27; 28; 29; 35; 36 right; 37; 48 top left; 51; 54 top right, top left, bottom left; 55; 61; 63; 71 left; 82 left; 82 bottom right; 83; 85; 88 top, center.